I0491328

CONFESSIONS OF A BLACK NERD PRESENTS:

BULLETS, BLUNTS AND BULLSHH! Vol#1

AN ADULT SKETCH/COLORING BOOK

BY SONNY CHIBA

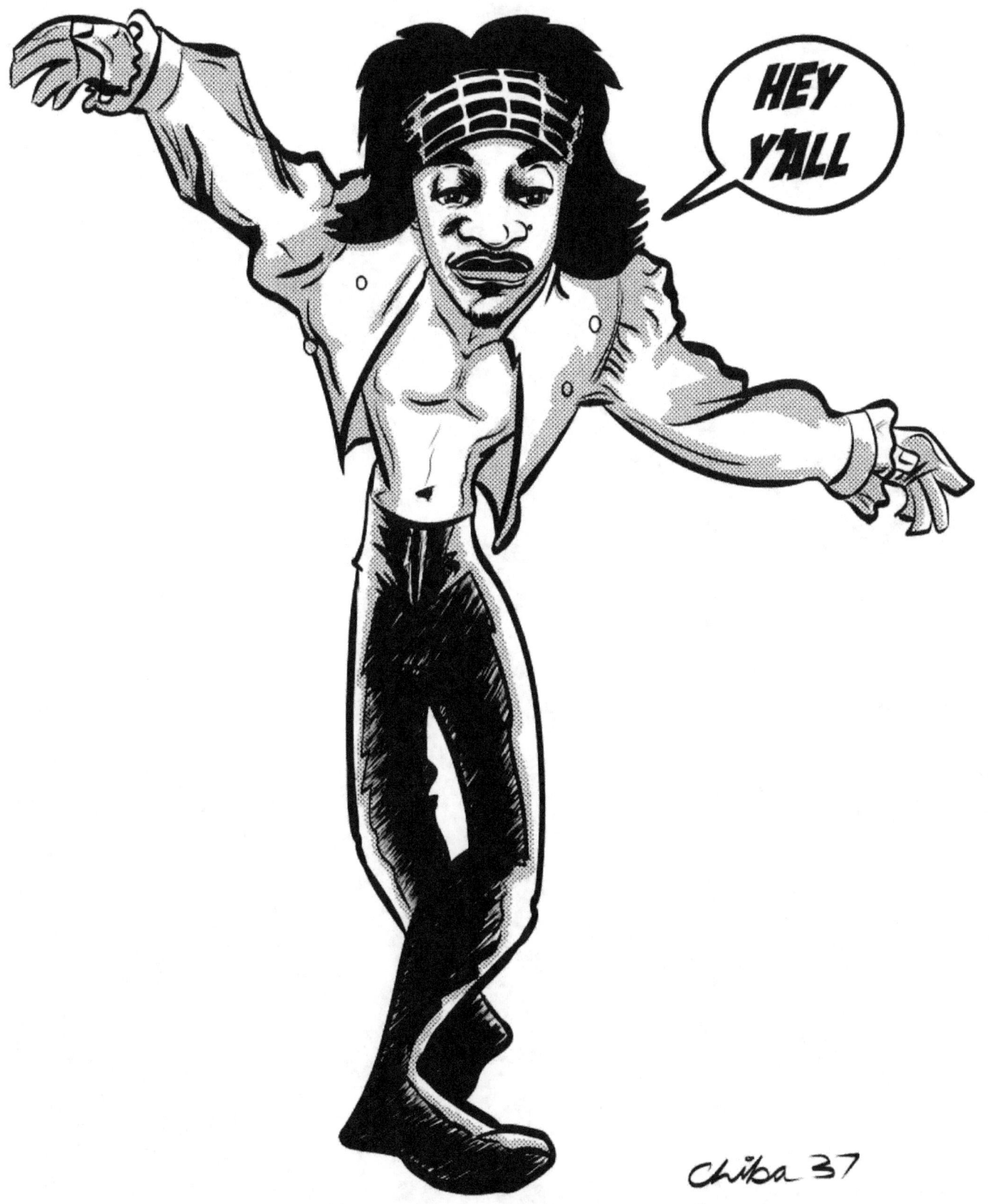

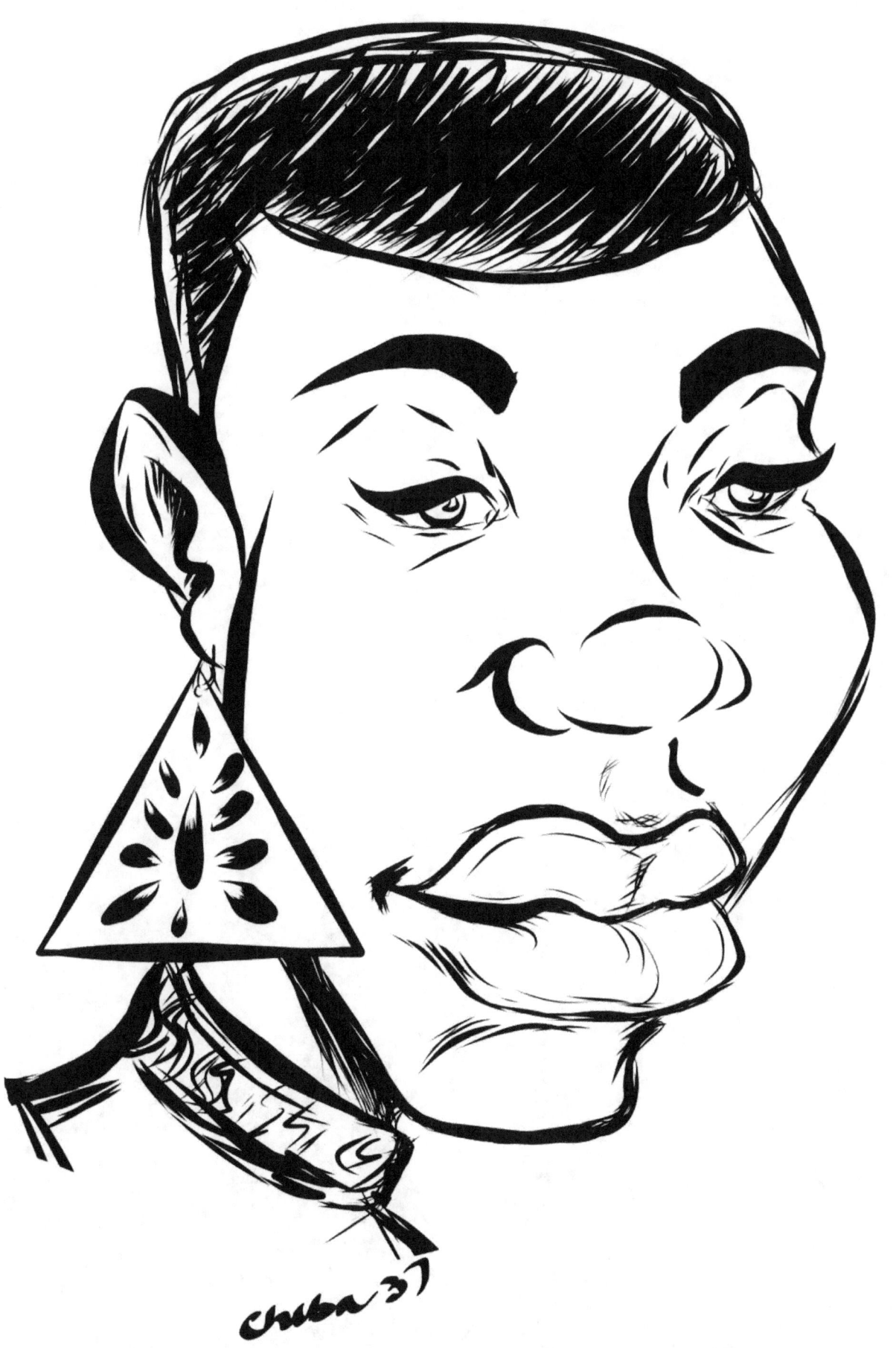

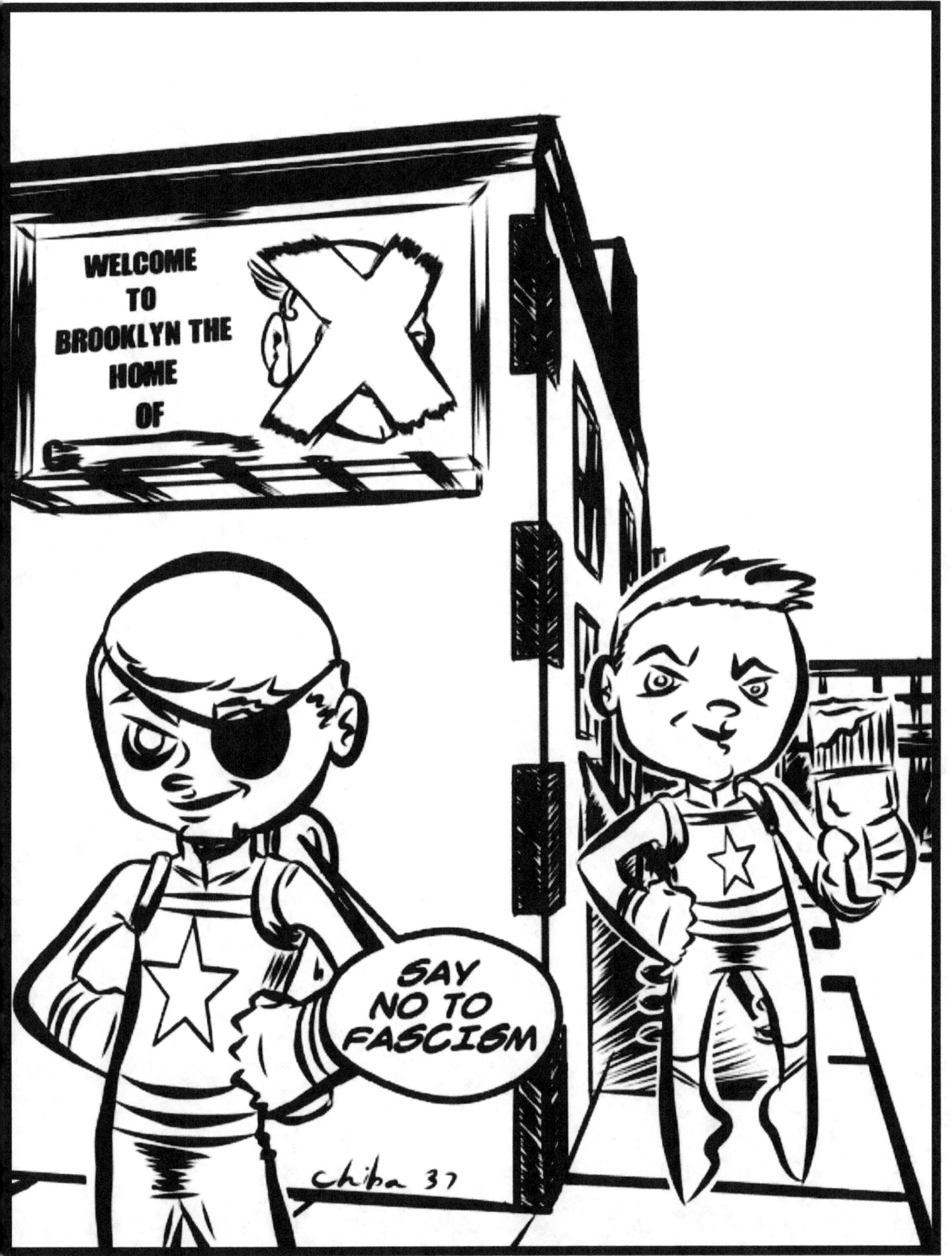

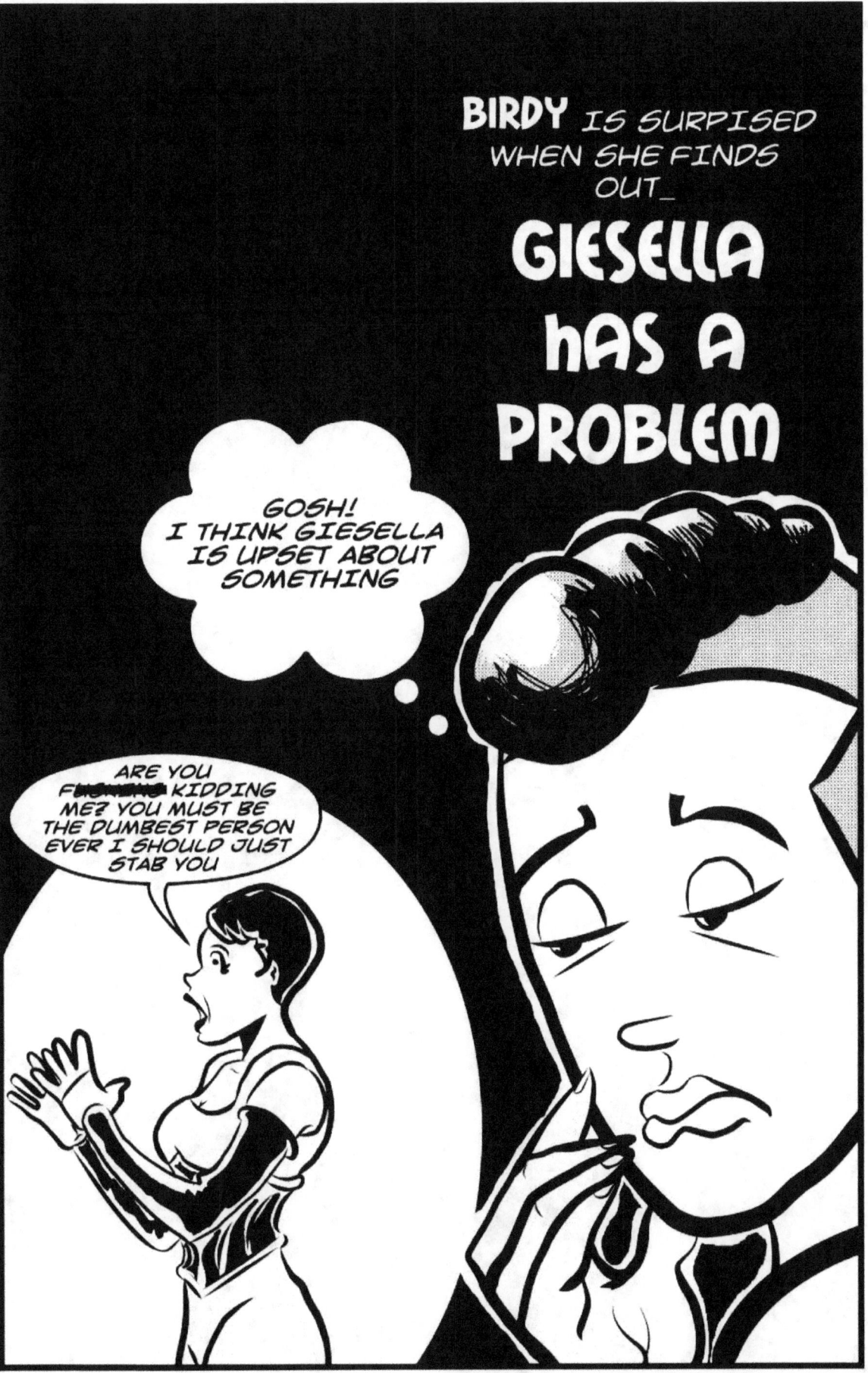

THE
W
O
M
A
N
IN RED

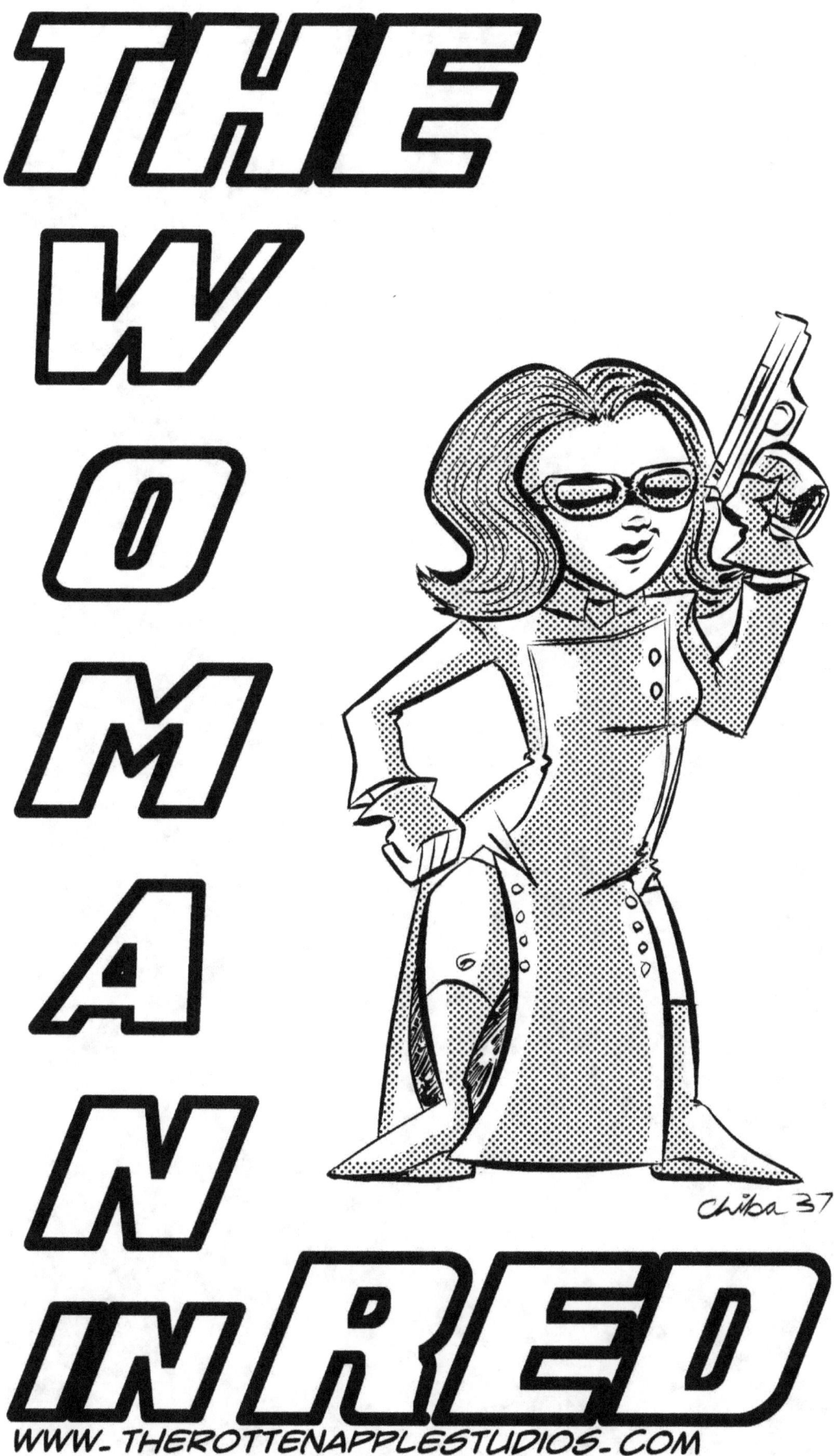

WWW. THEROTTENAPPLESTUDIOS.COM

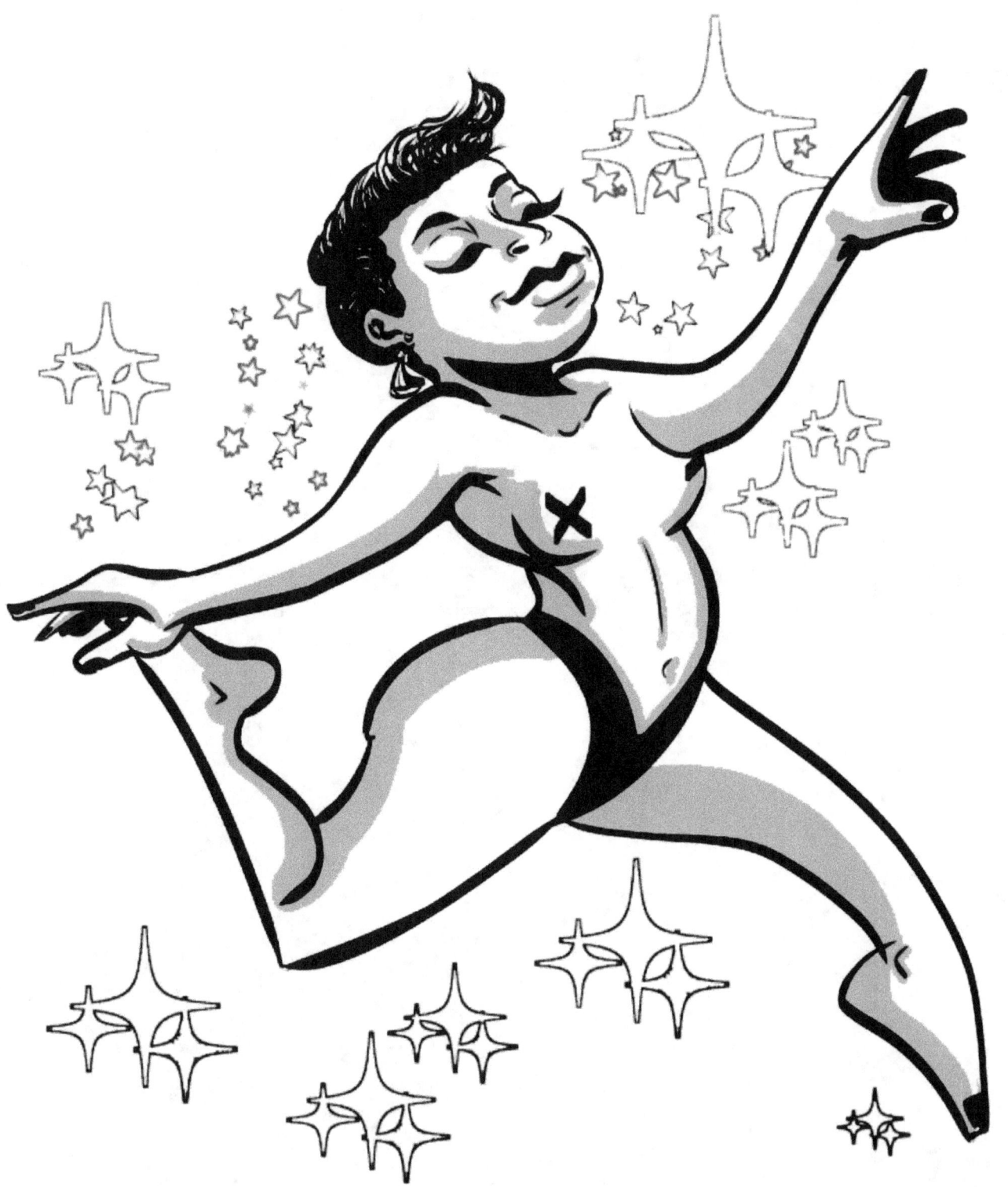

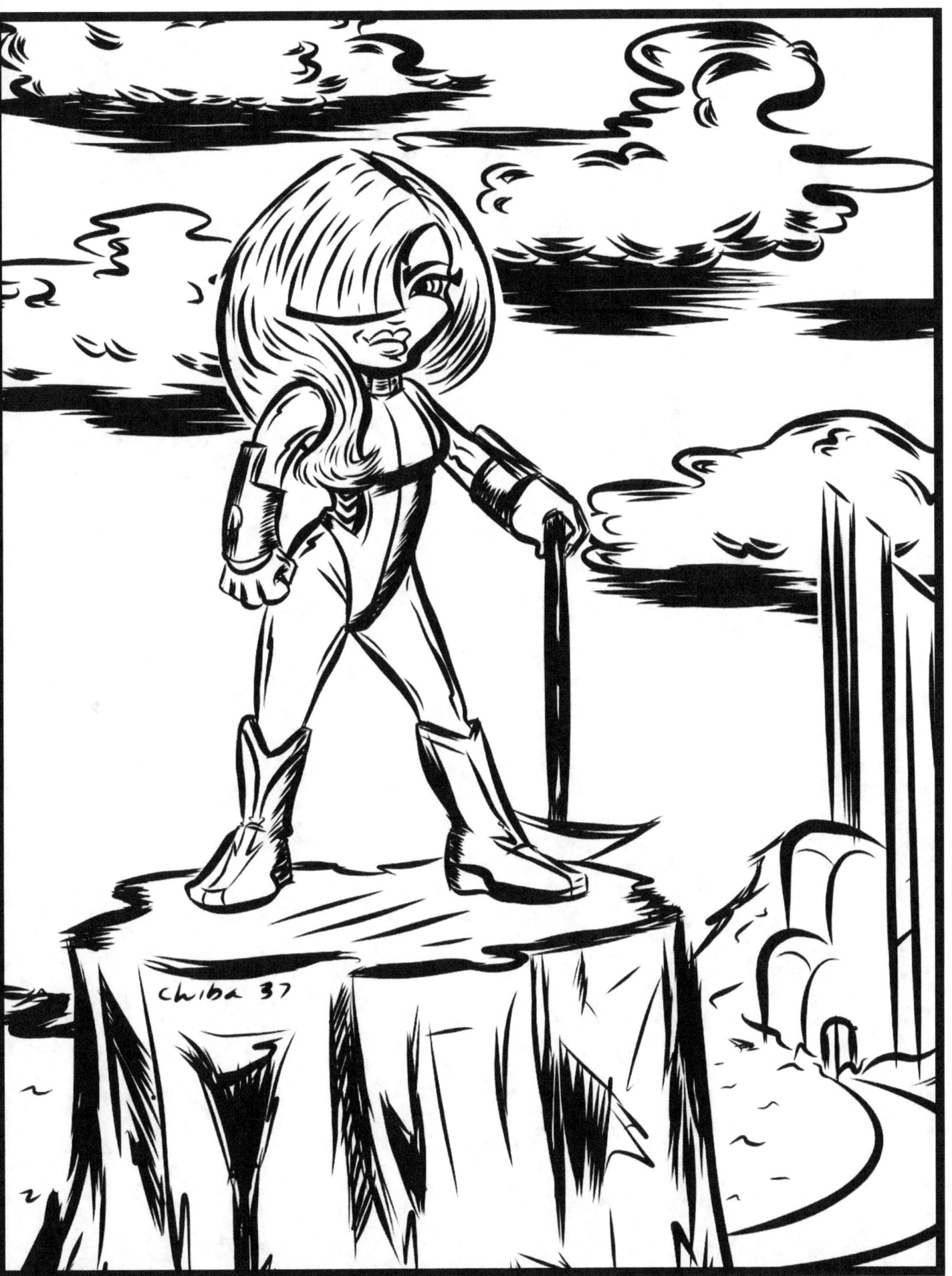

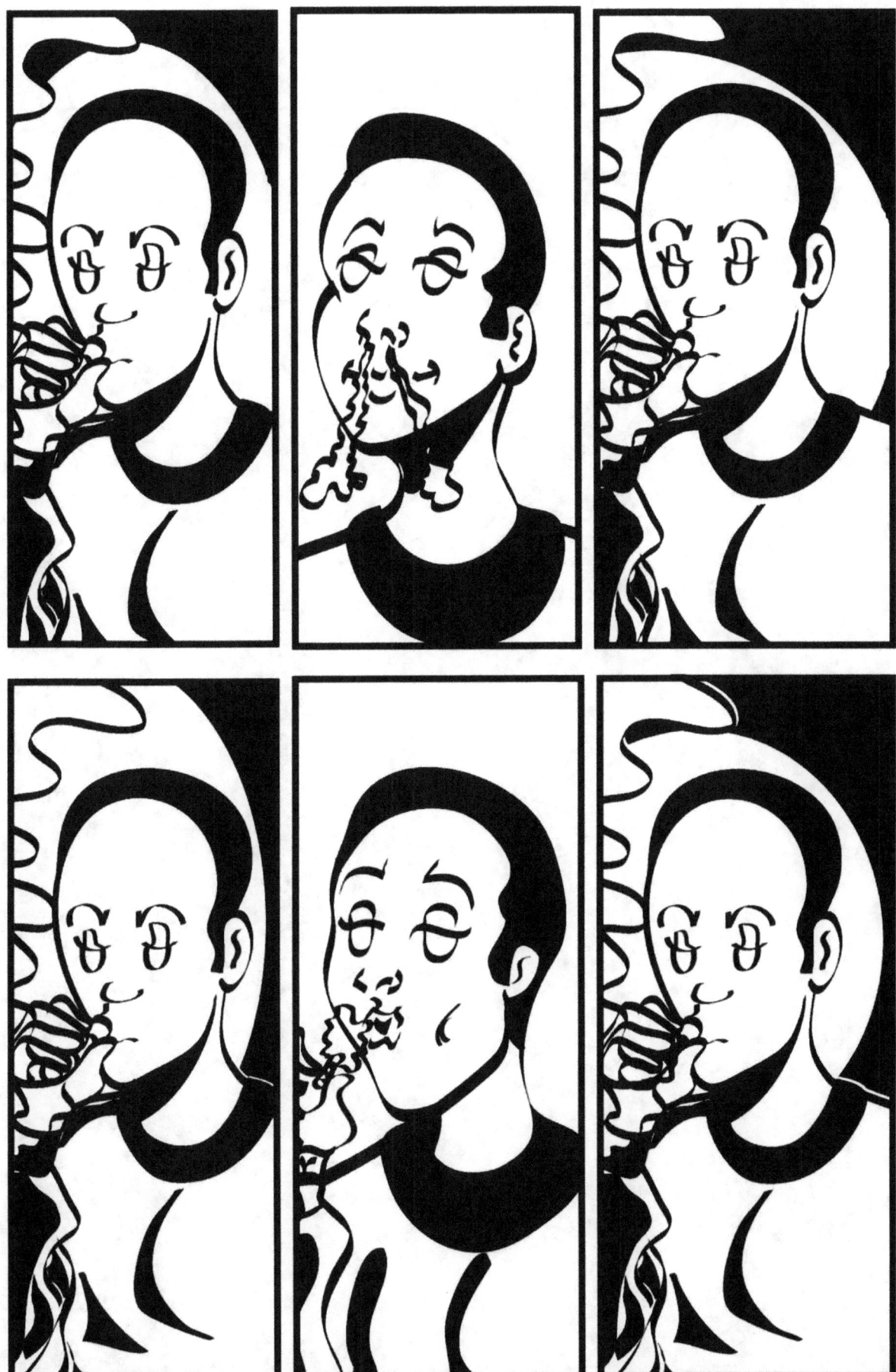

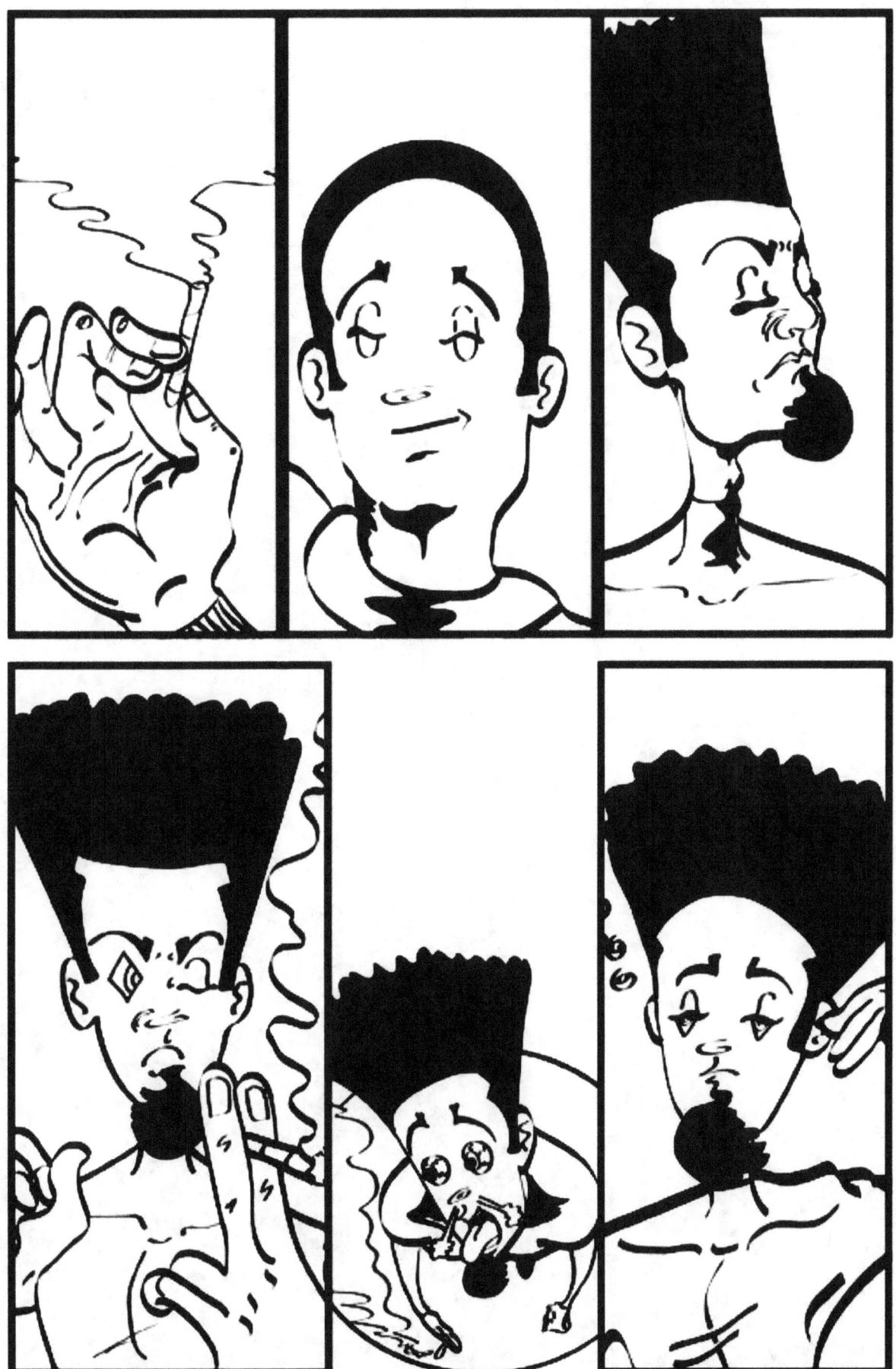

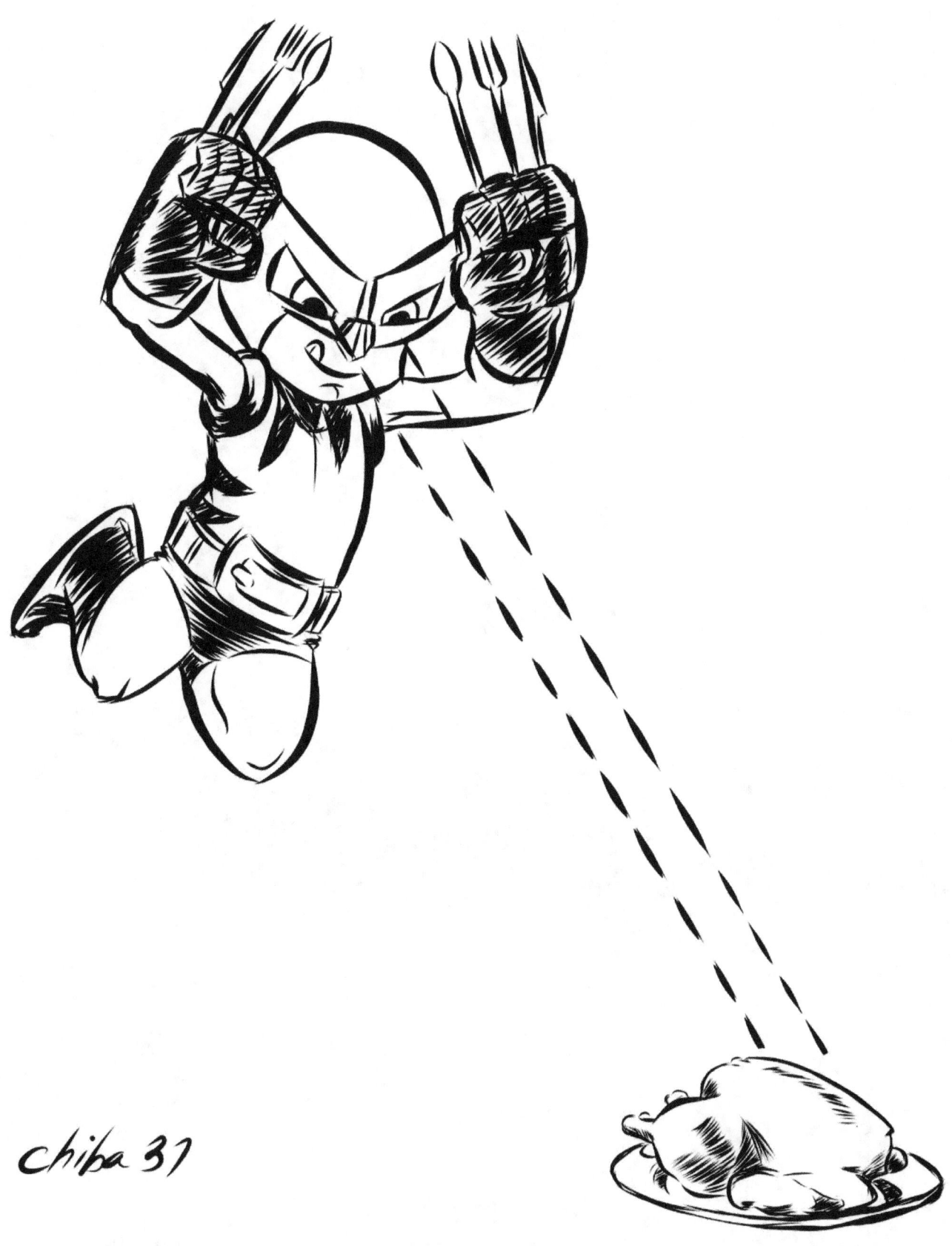

chiba 31

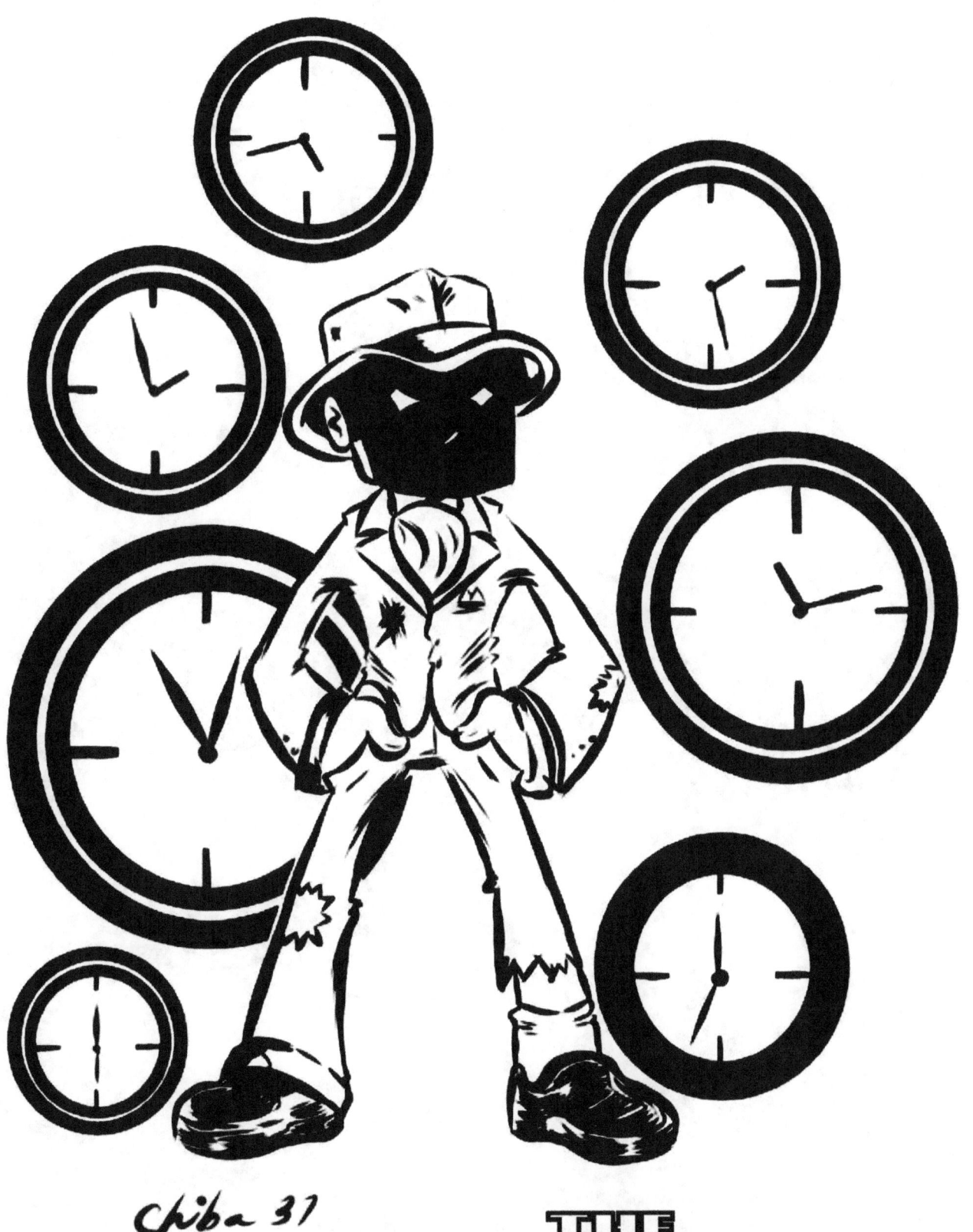

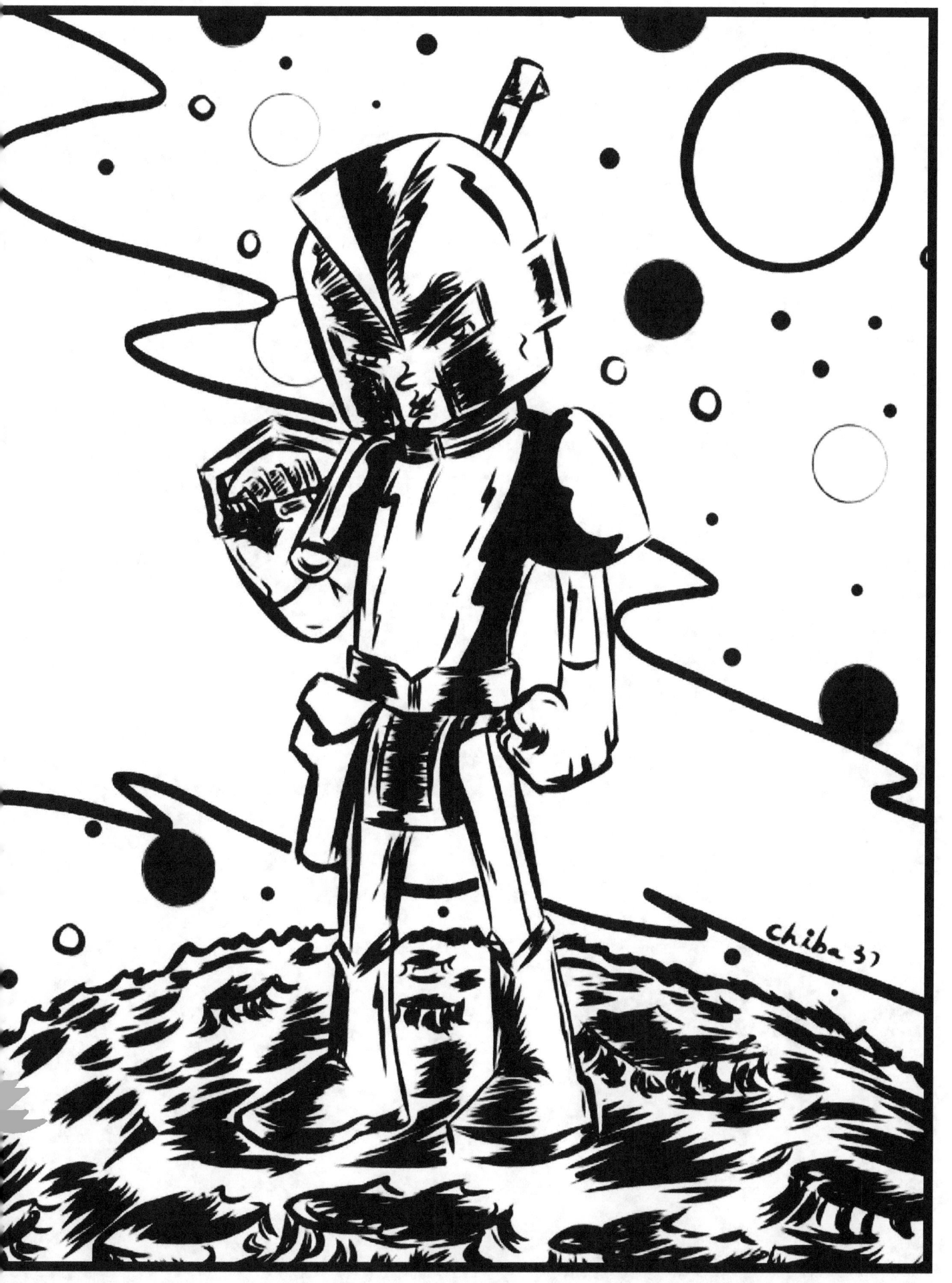

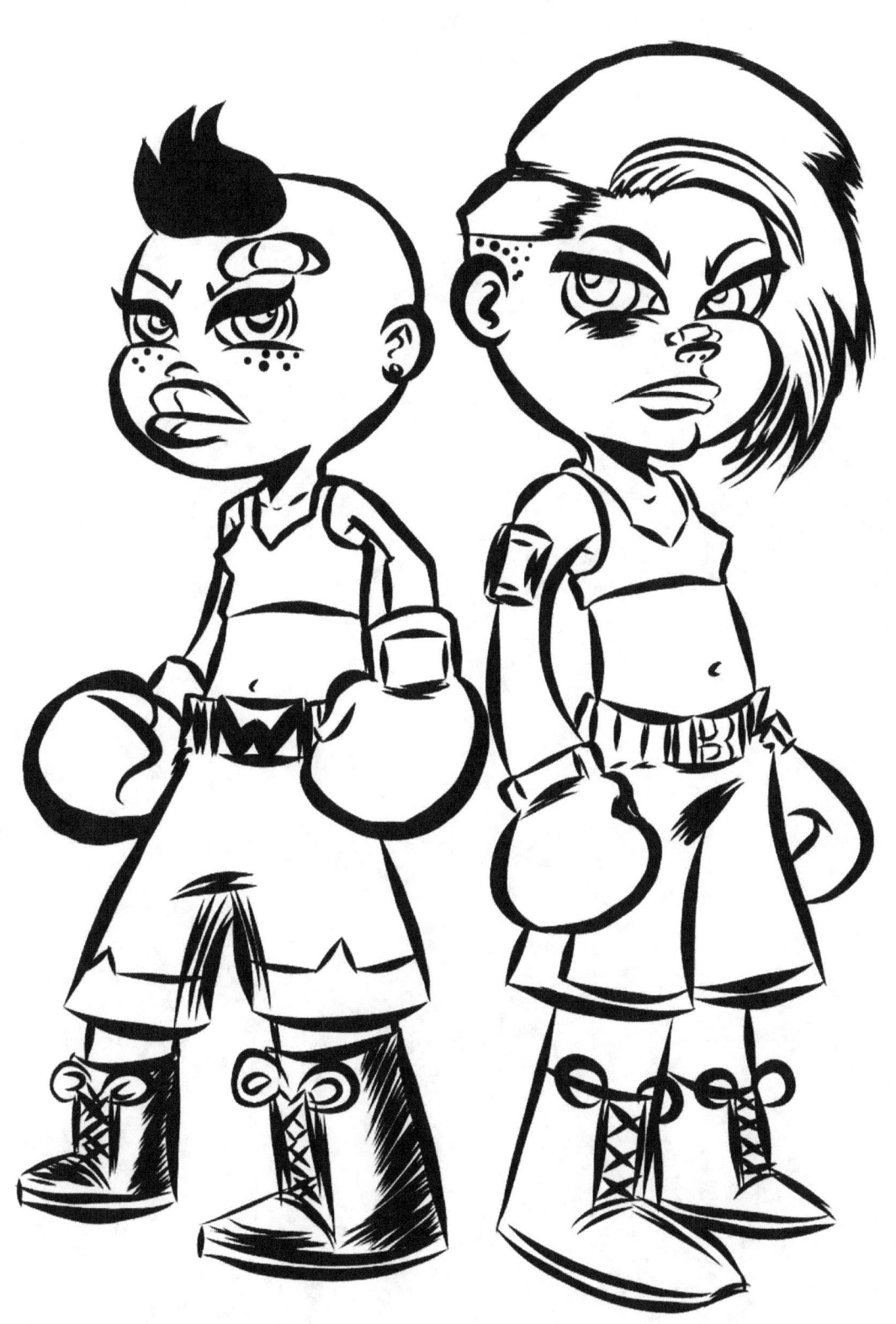

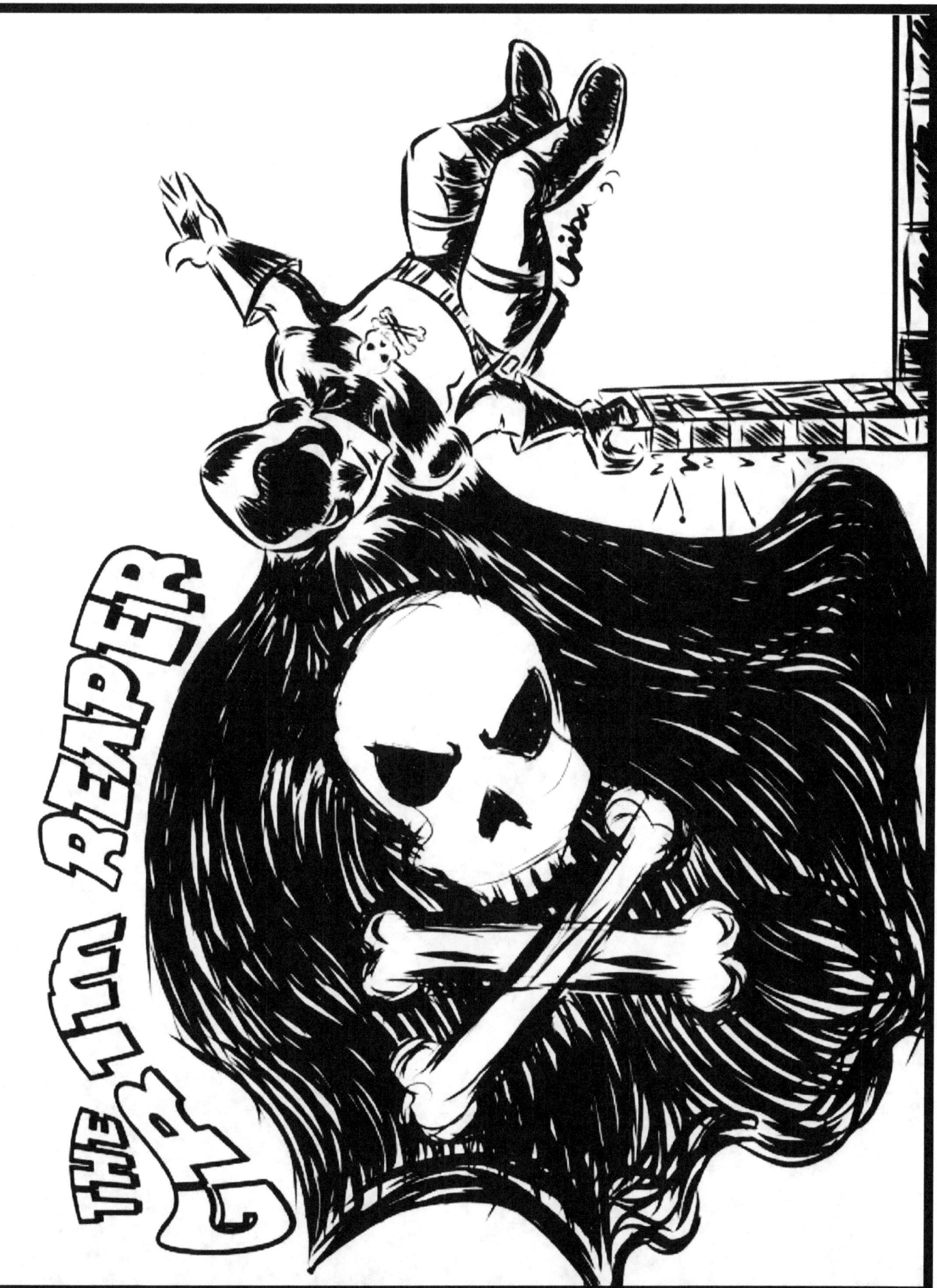

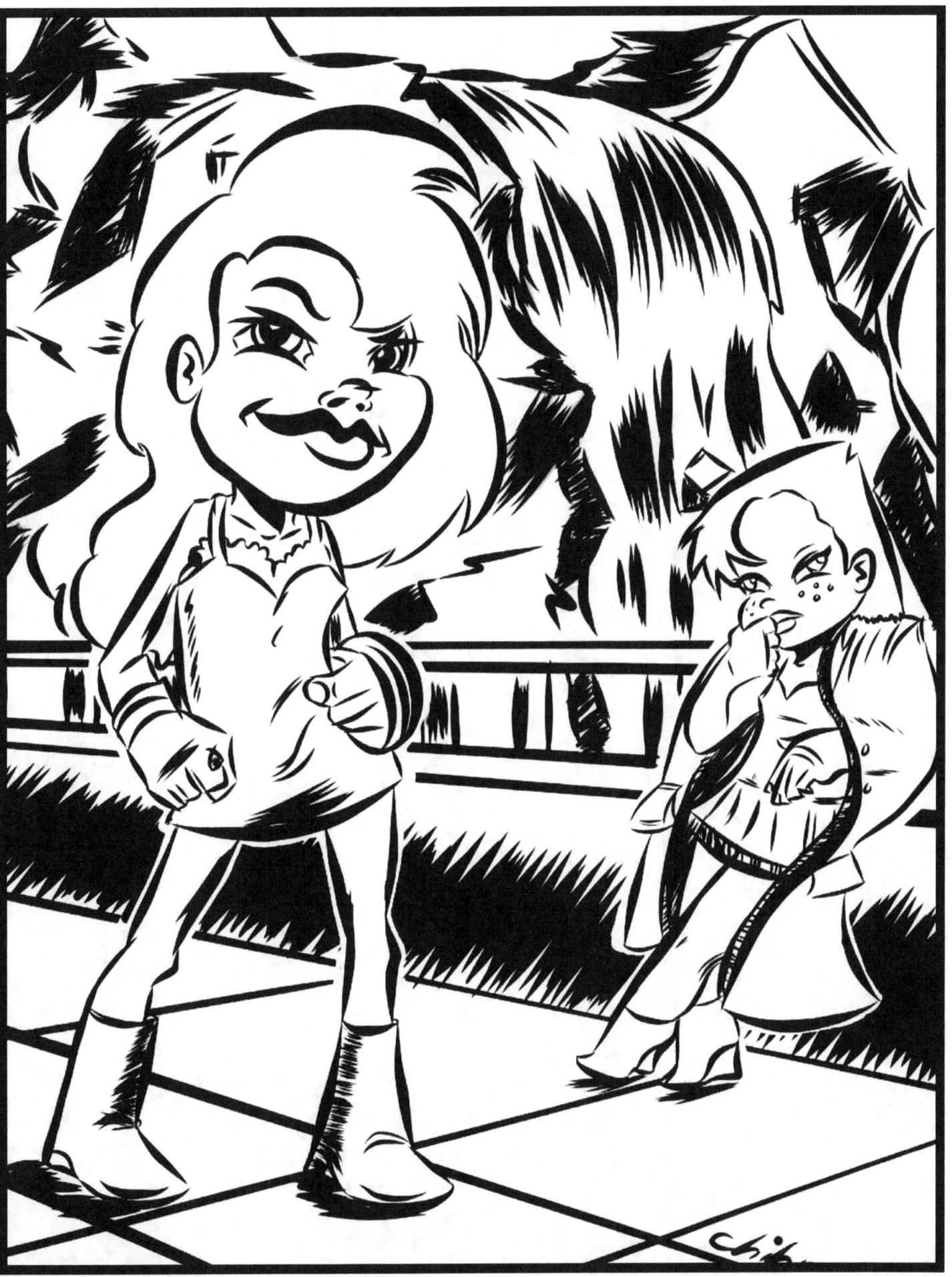

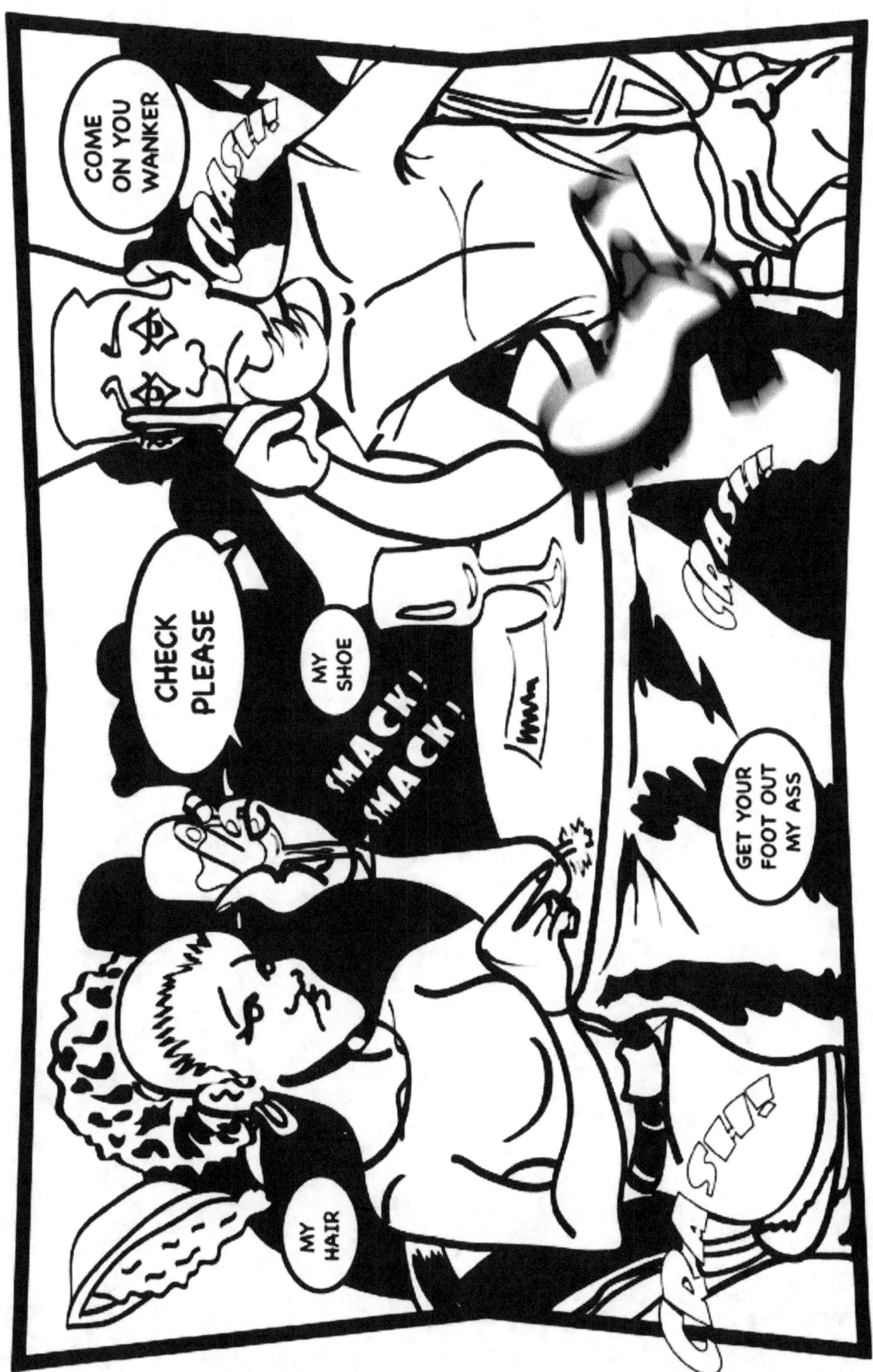

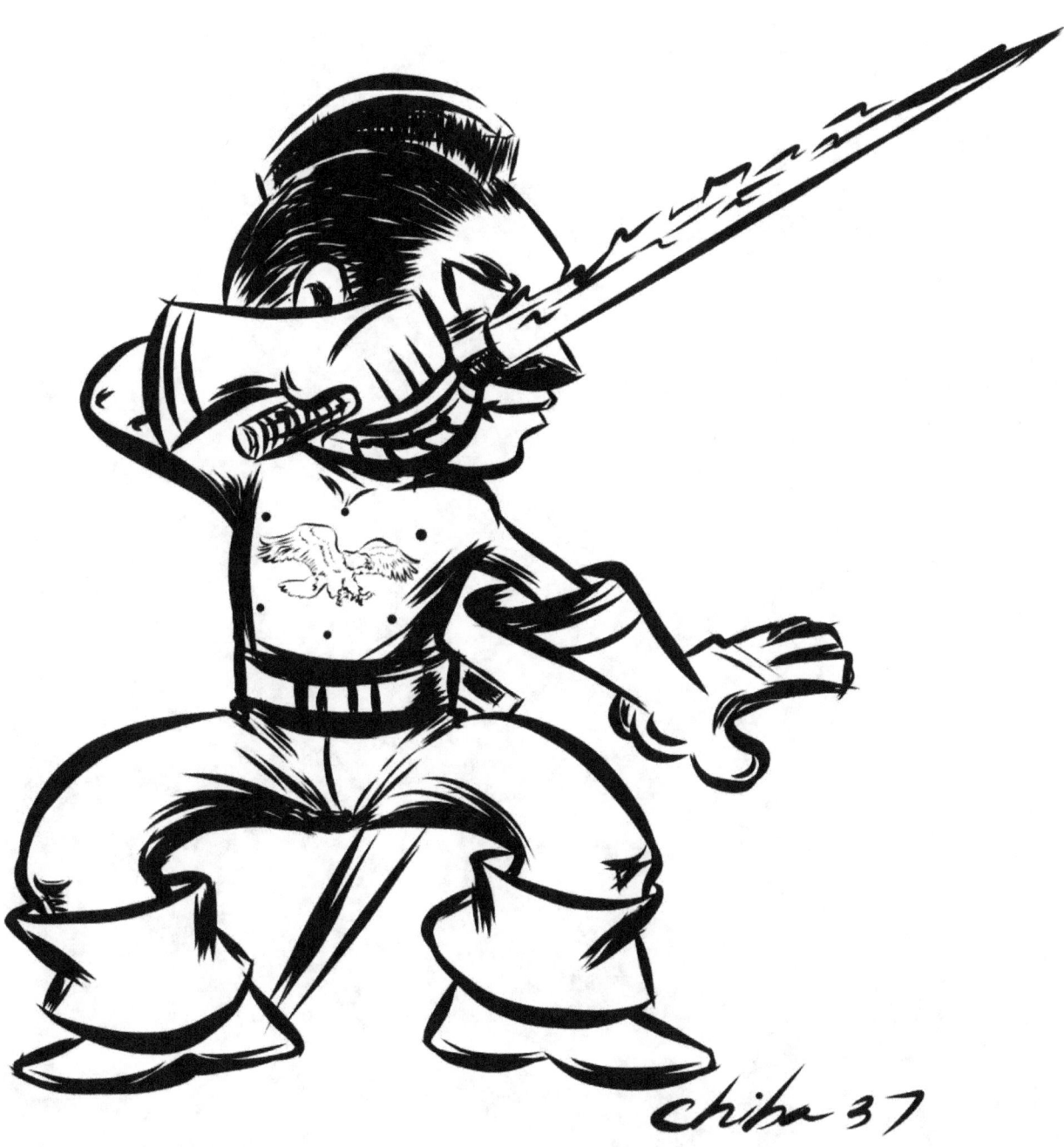

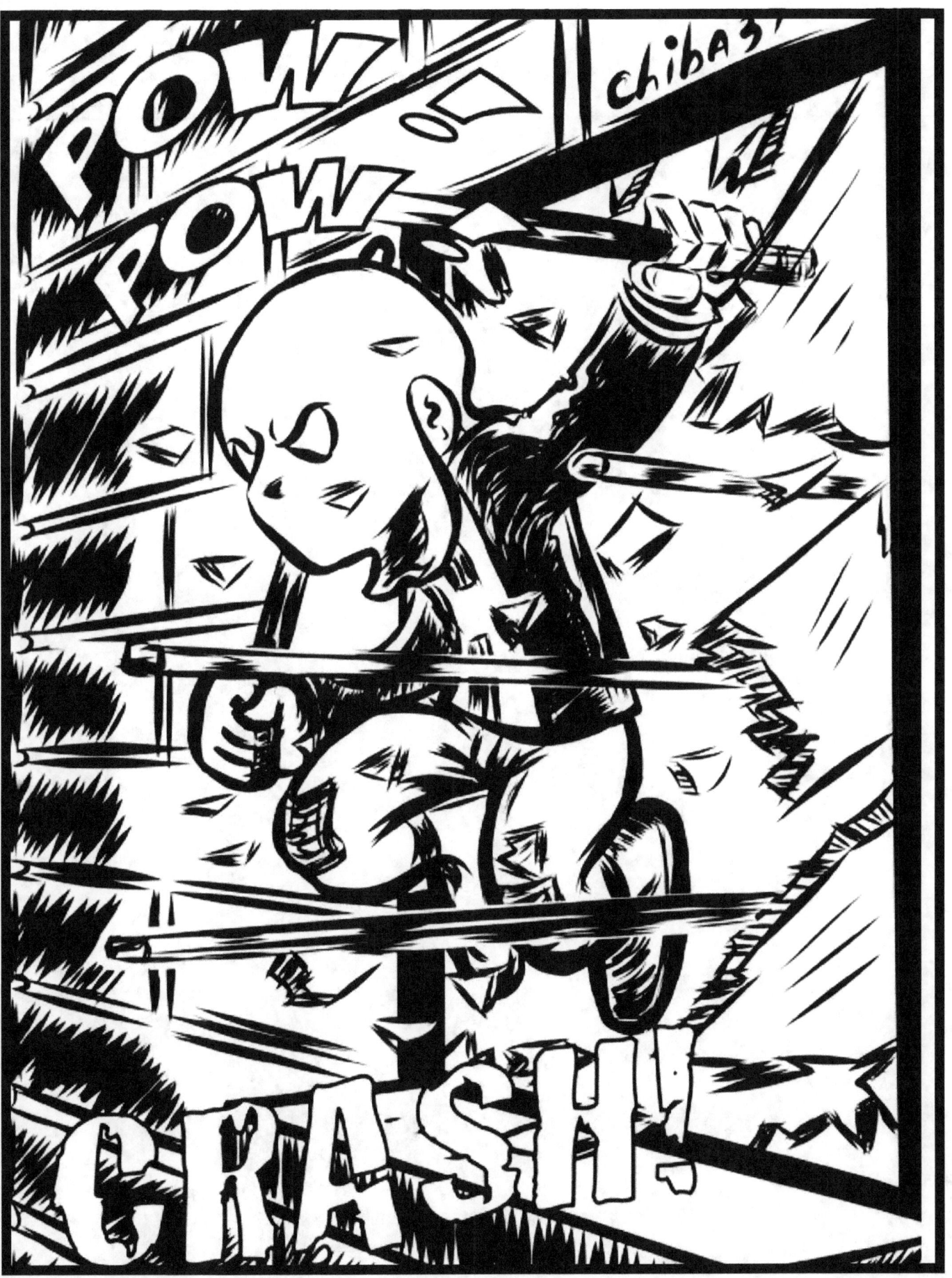

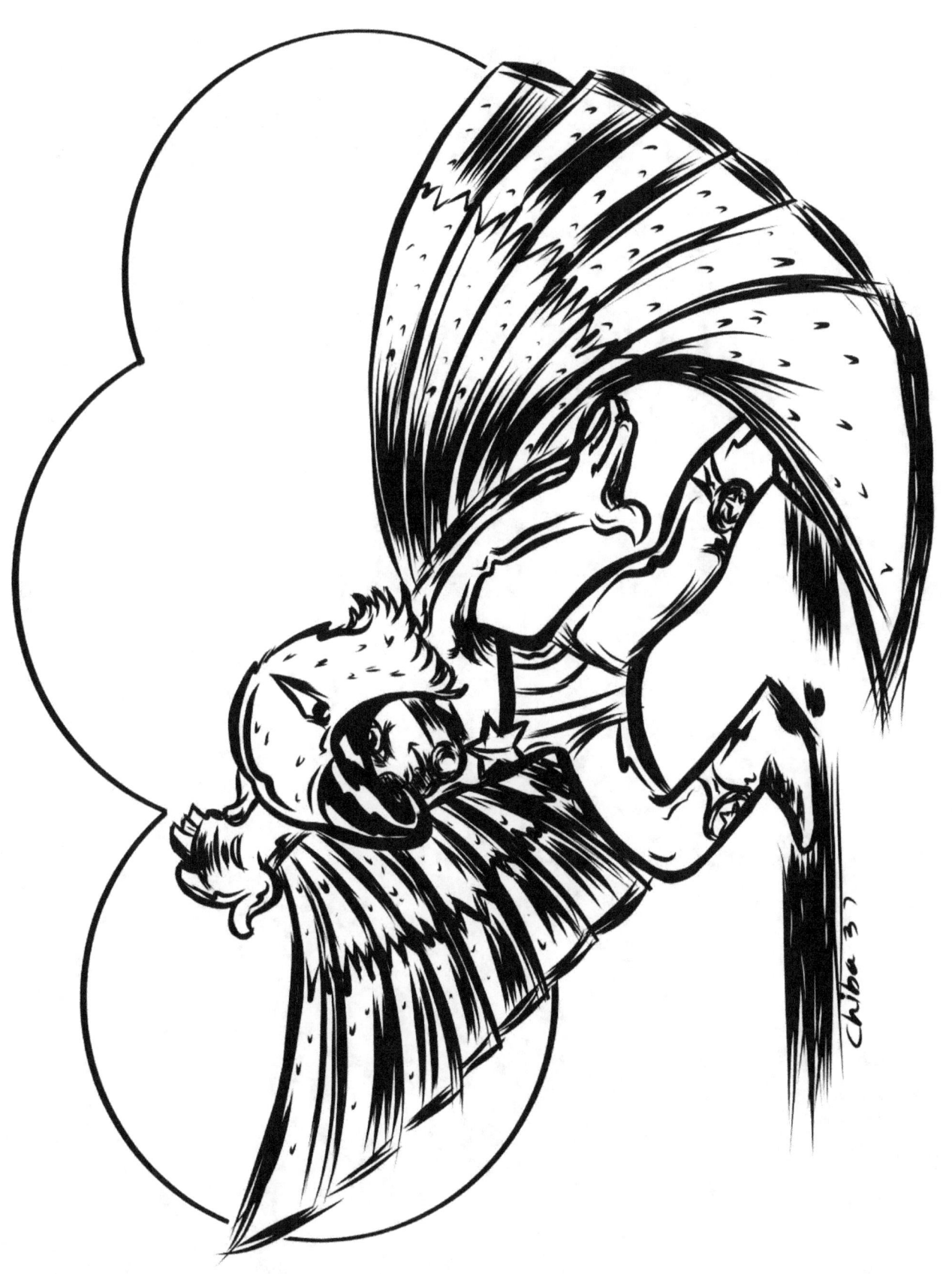

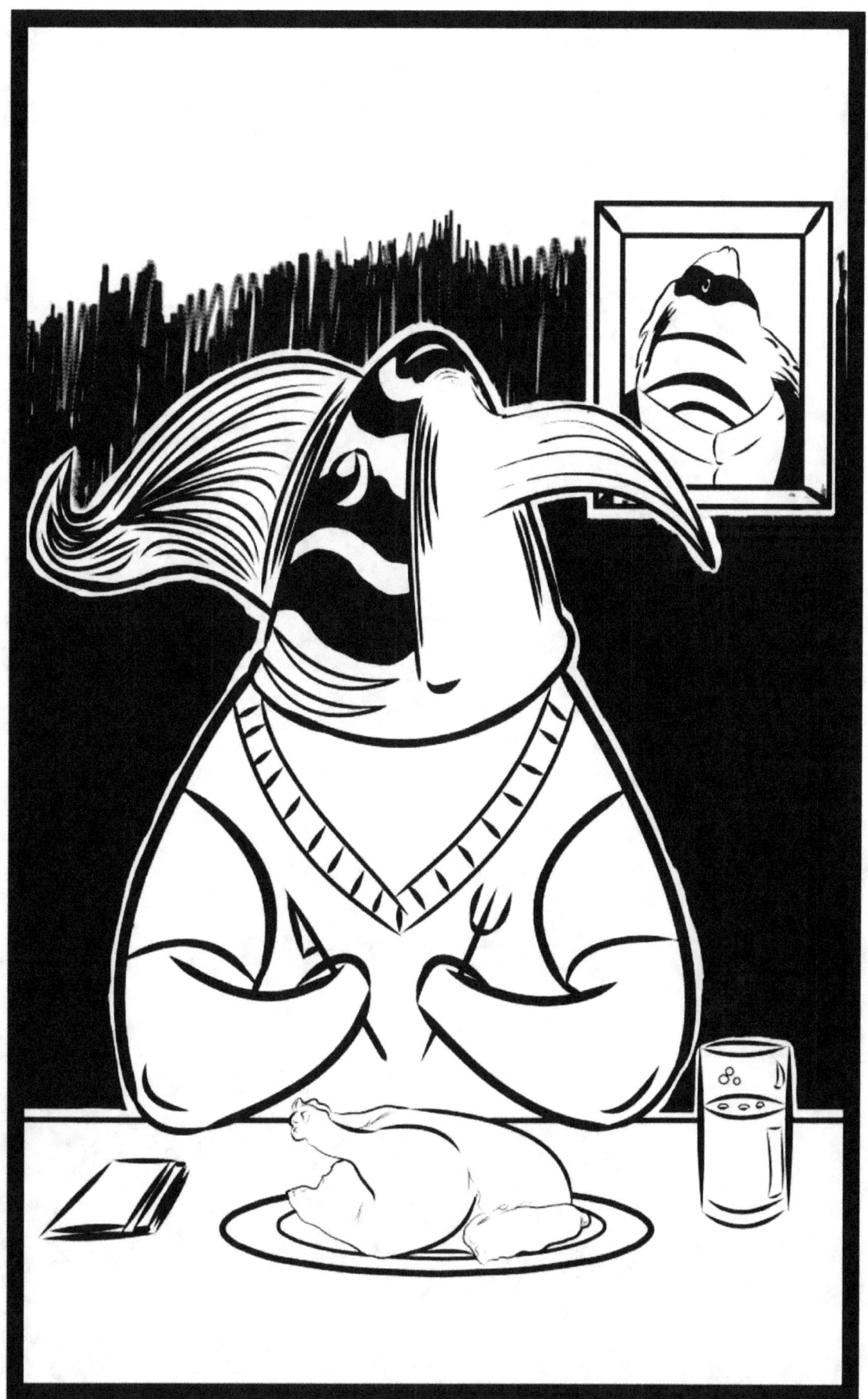

CHIBA 37

11-16-14

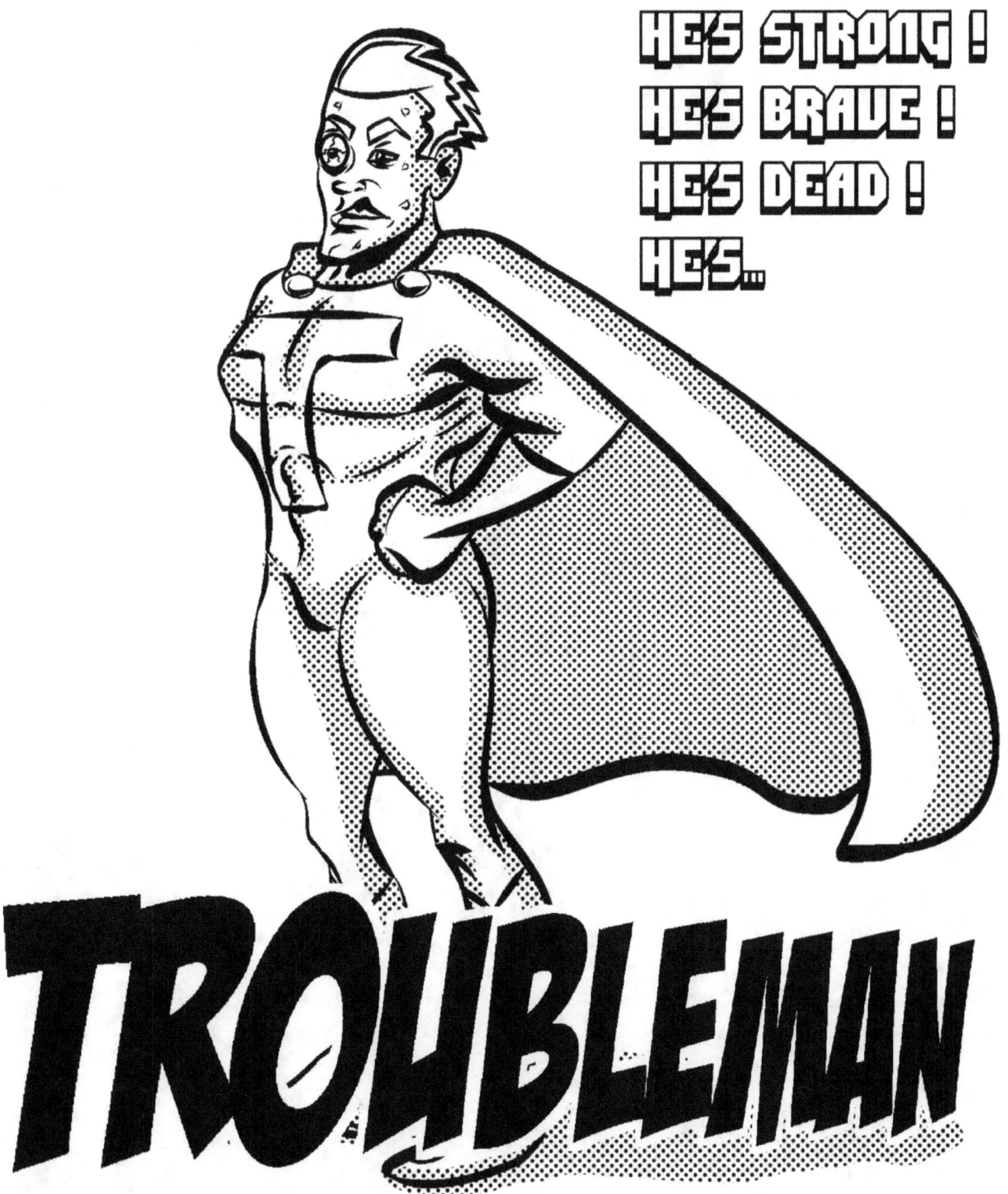

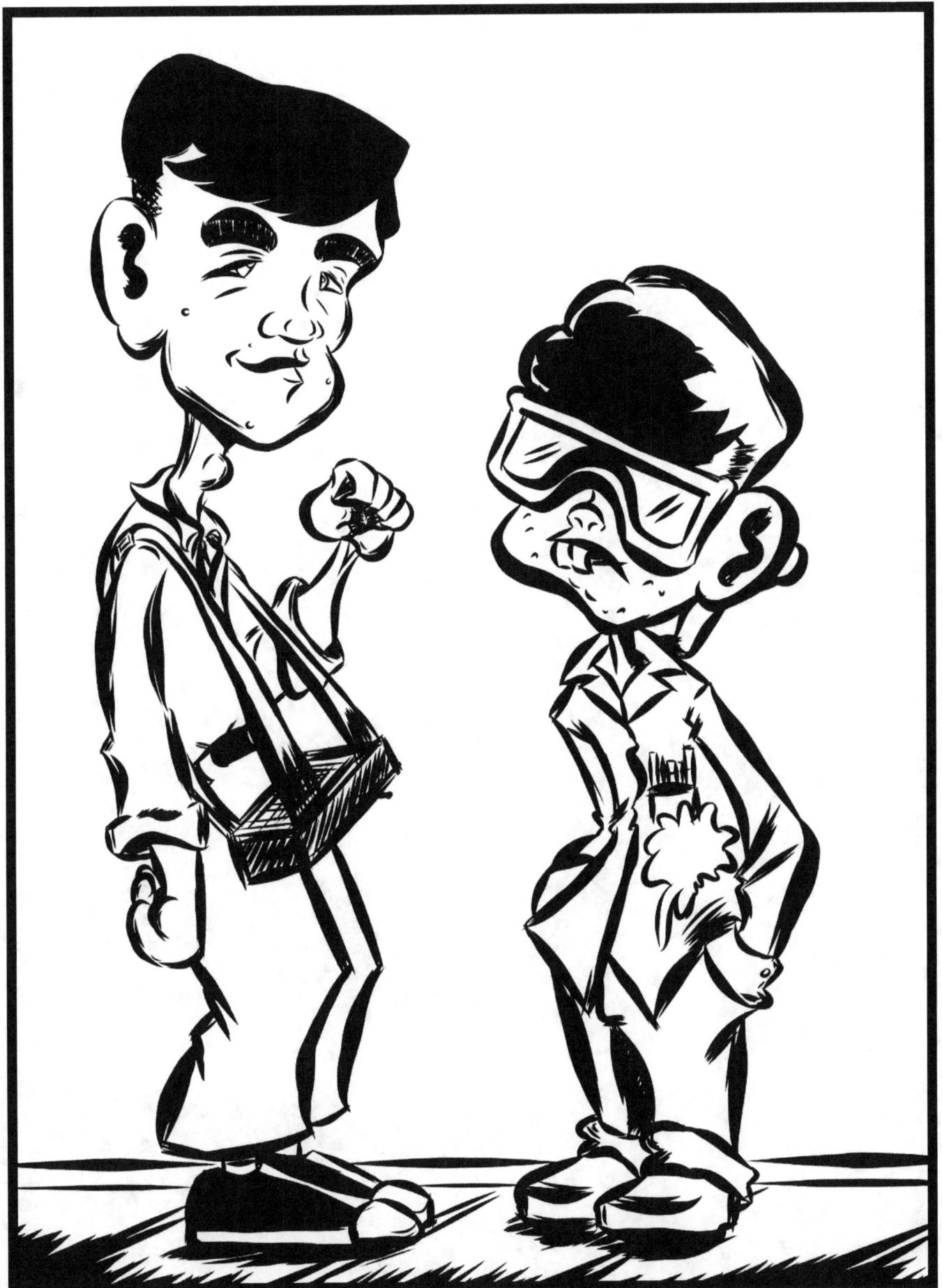

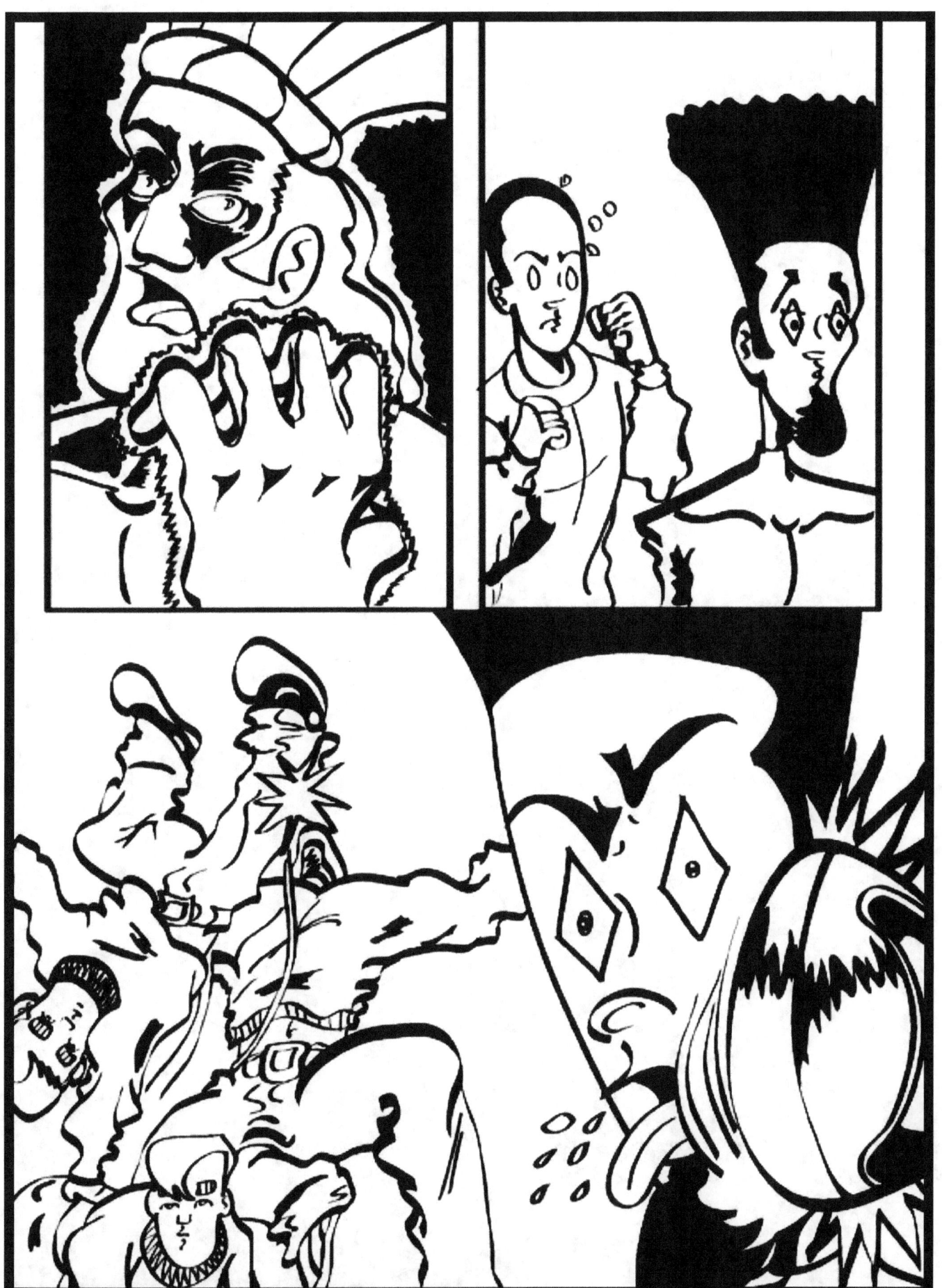

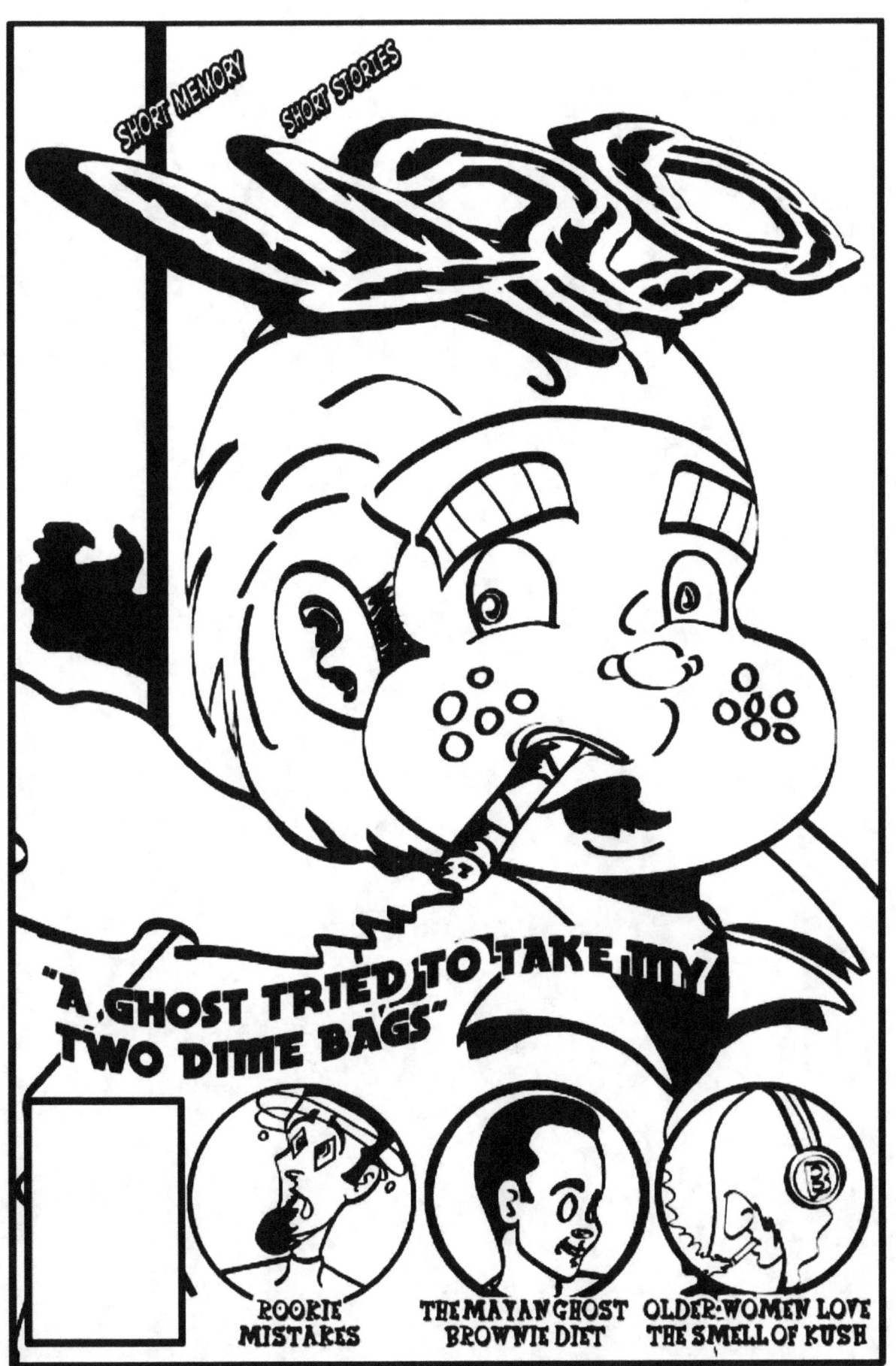

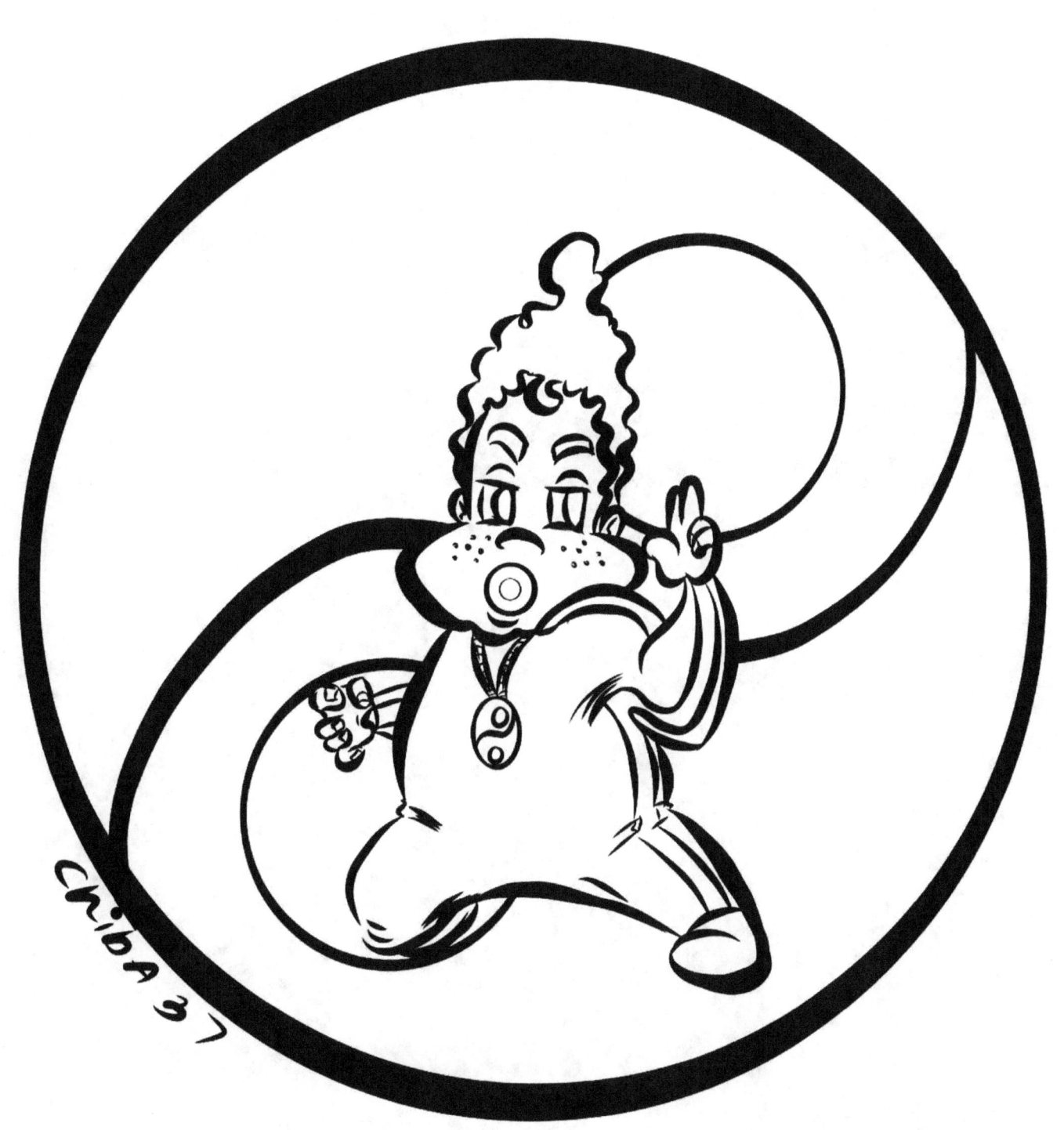

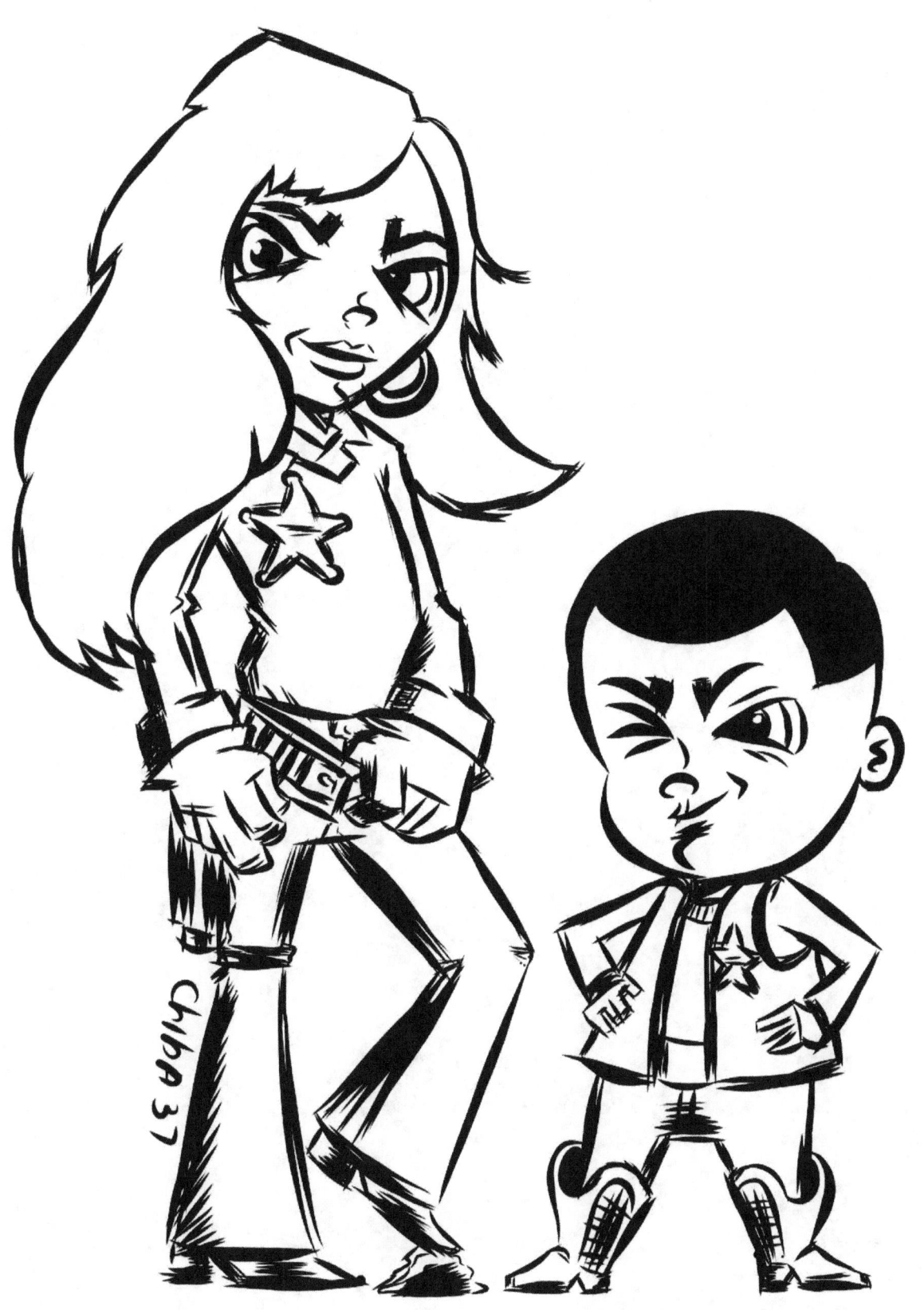

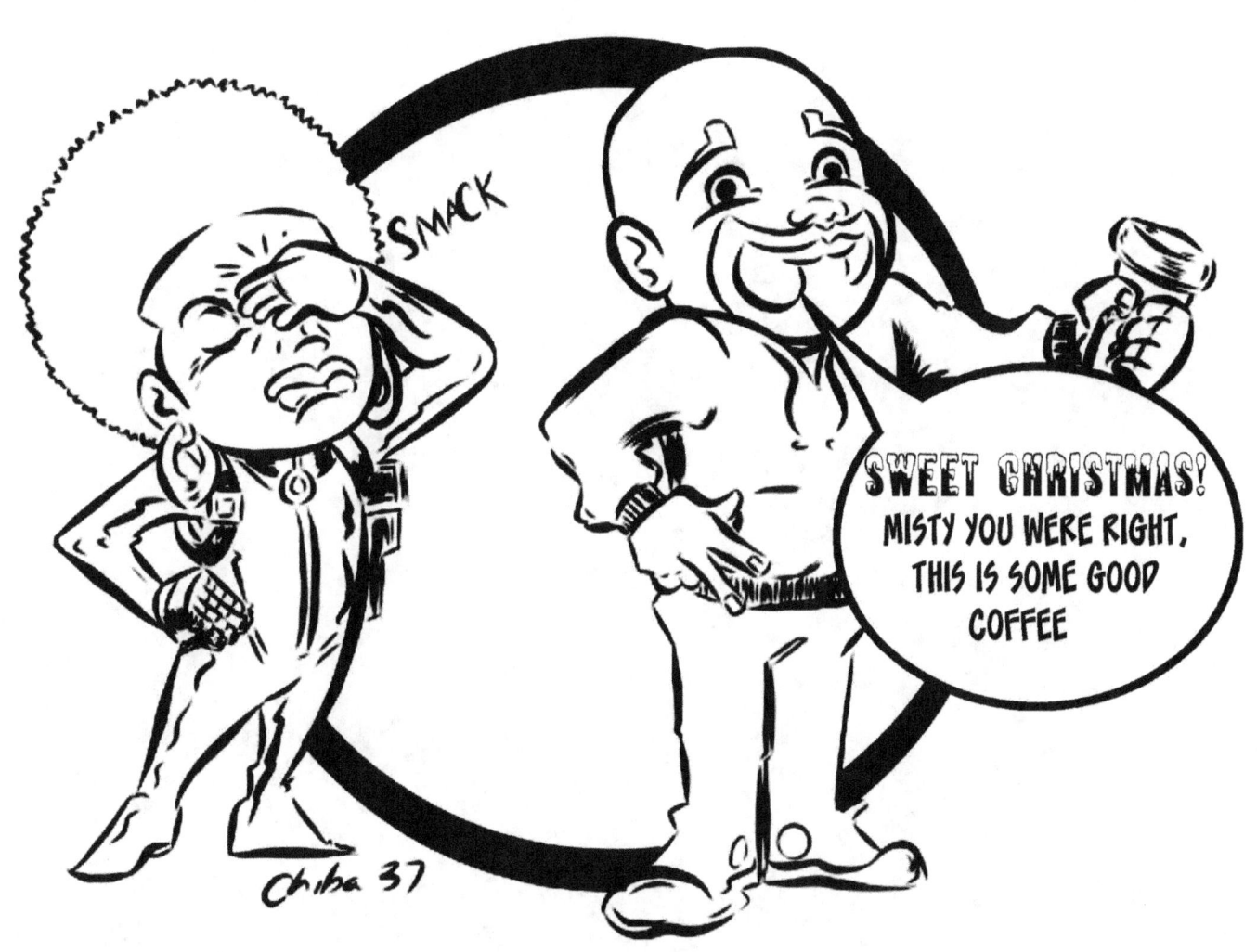

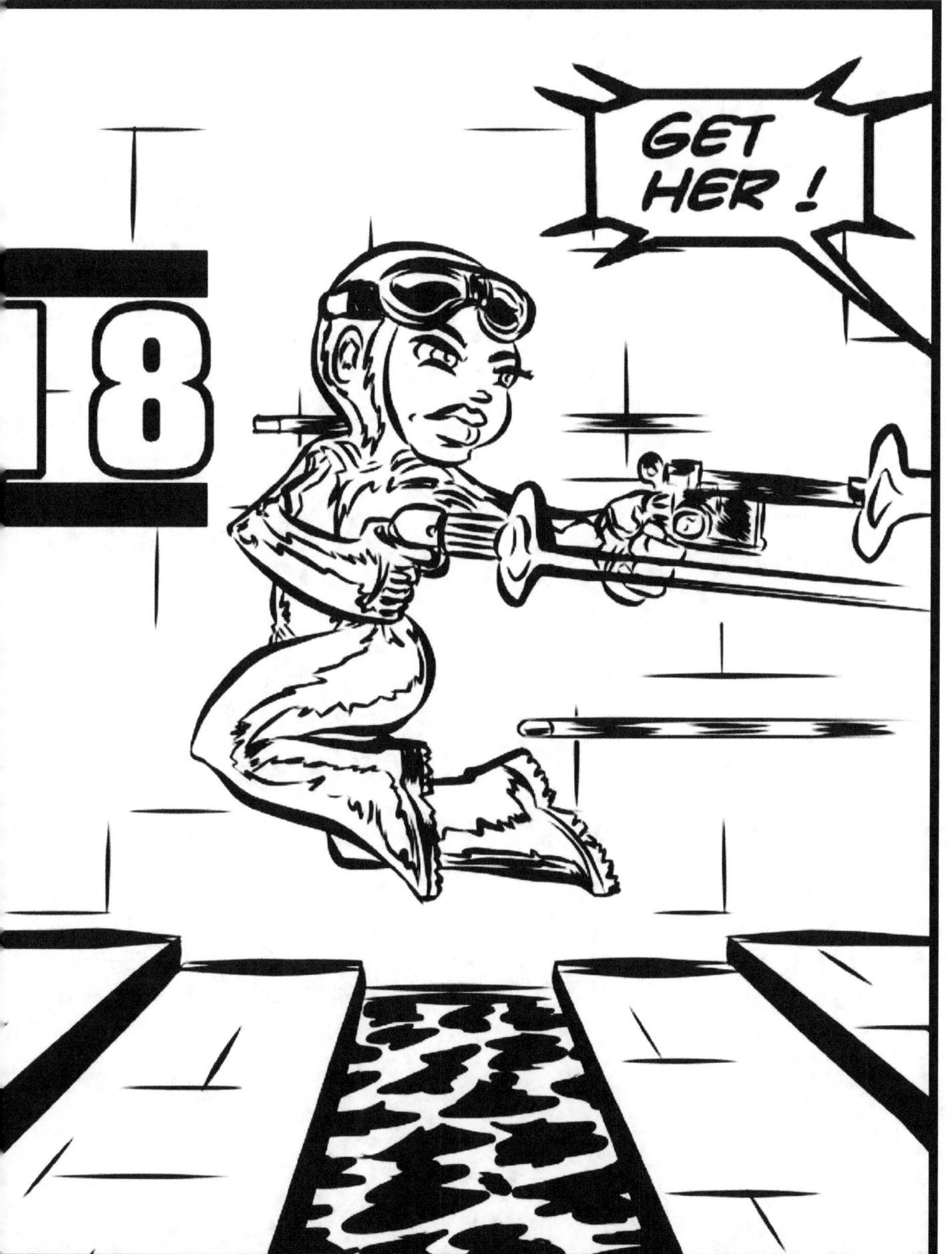

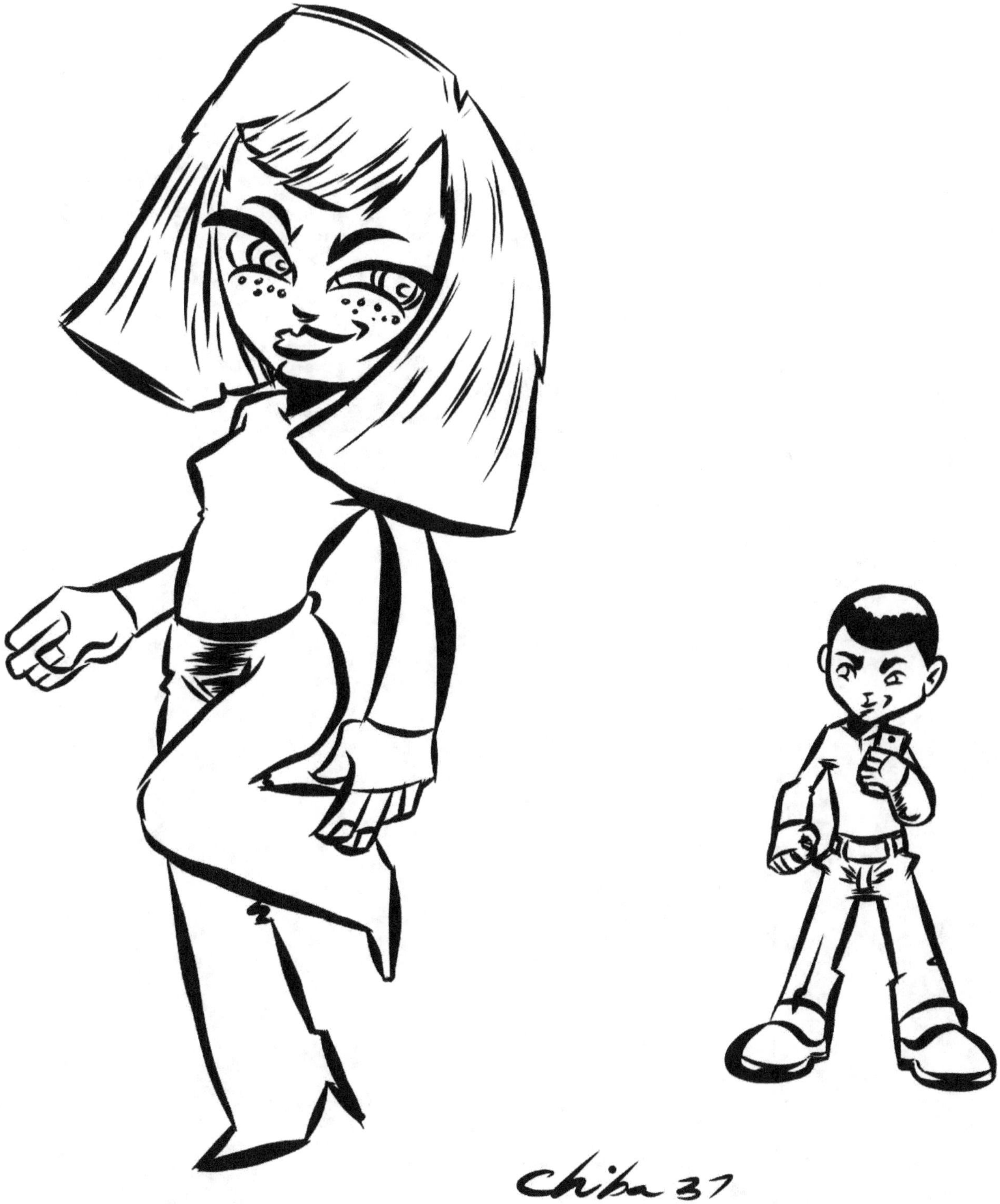

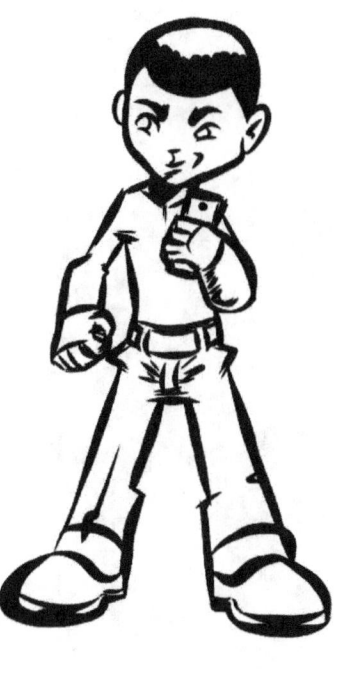

chiba 37

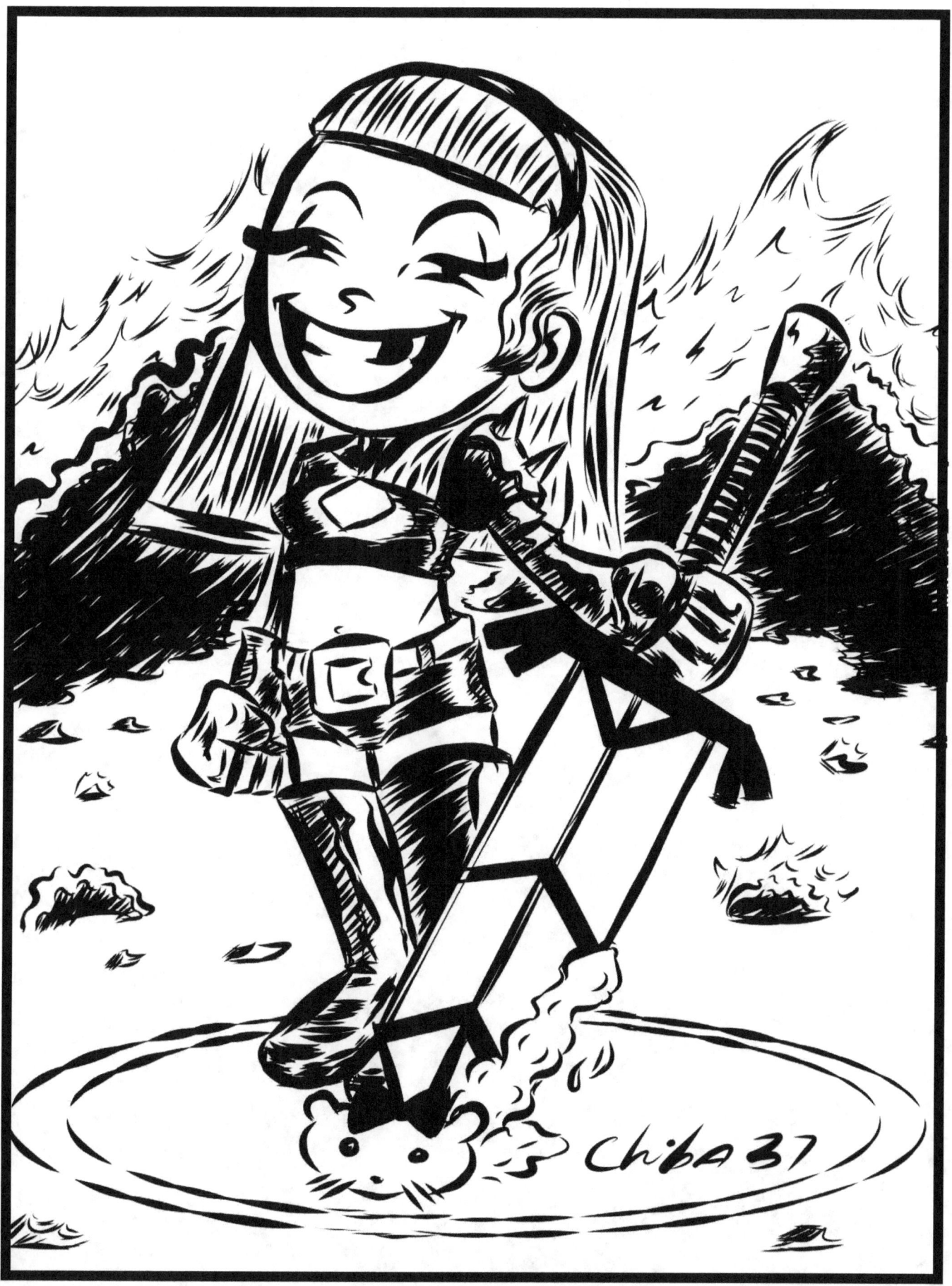

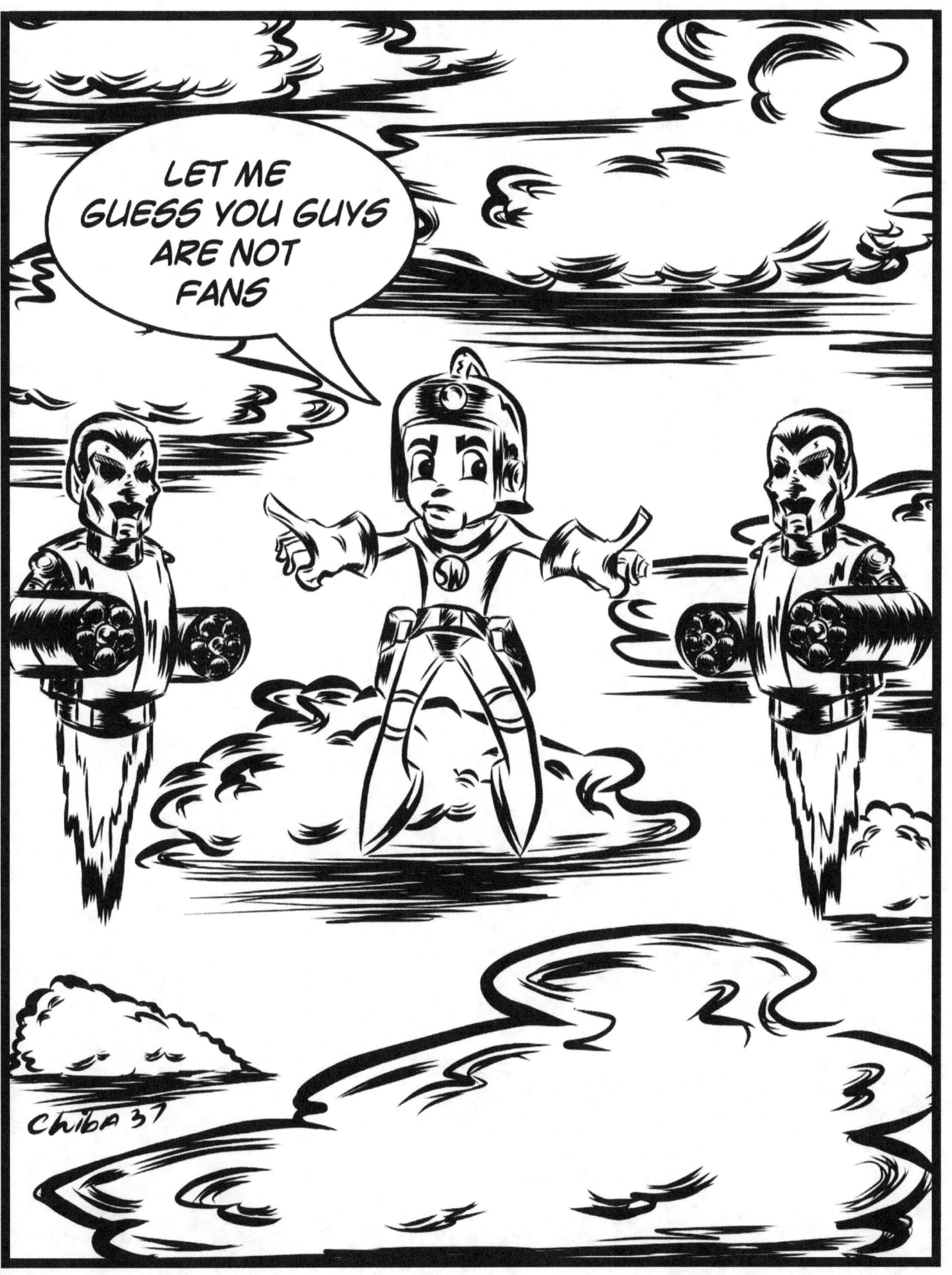

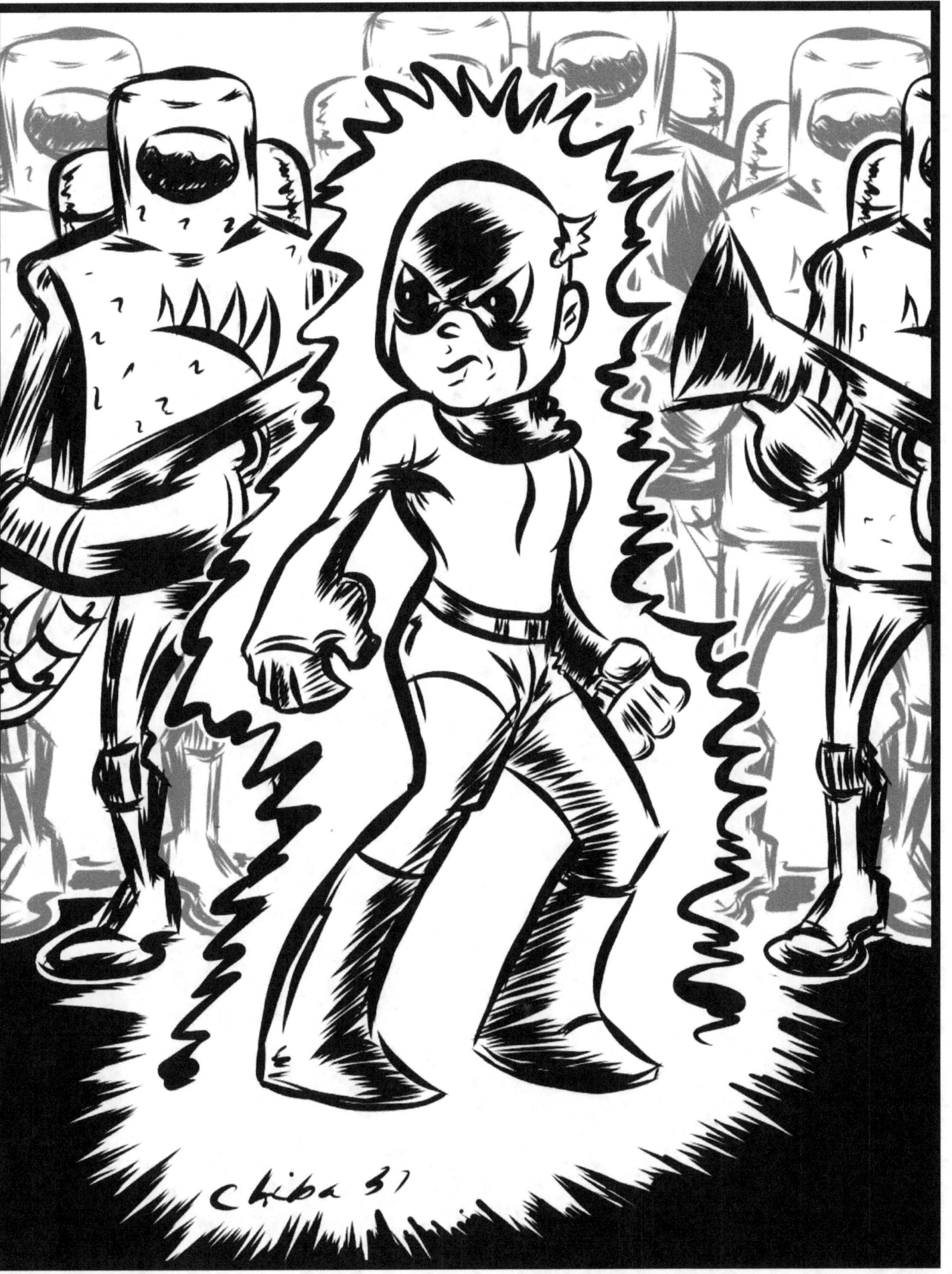

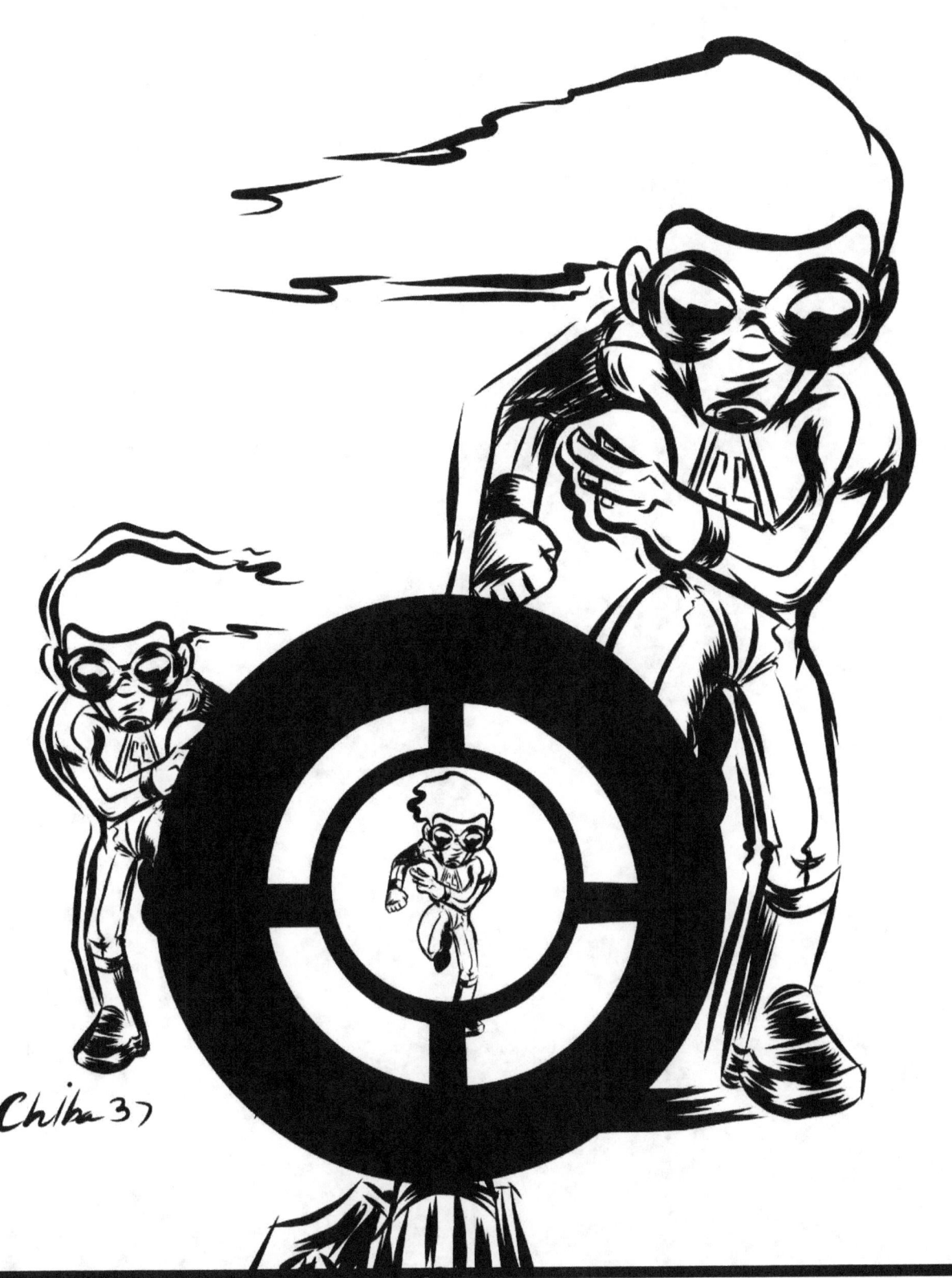

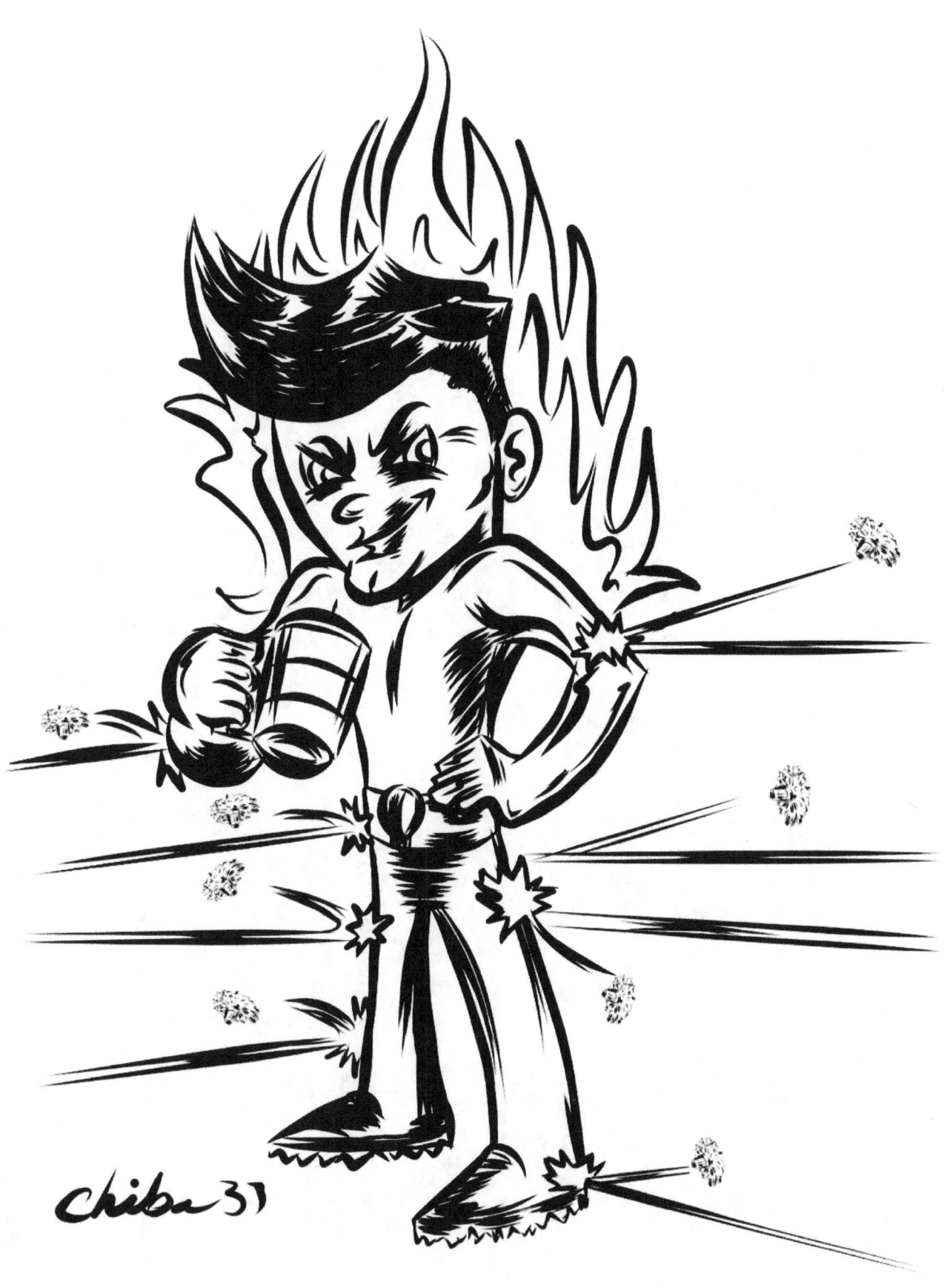

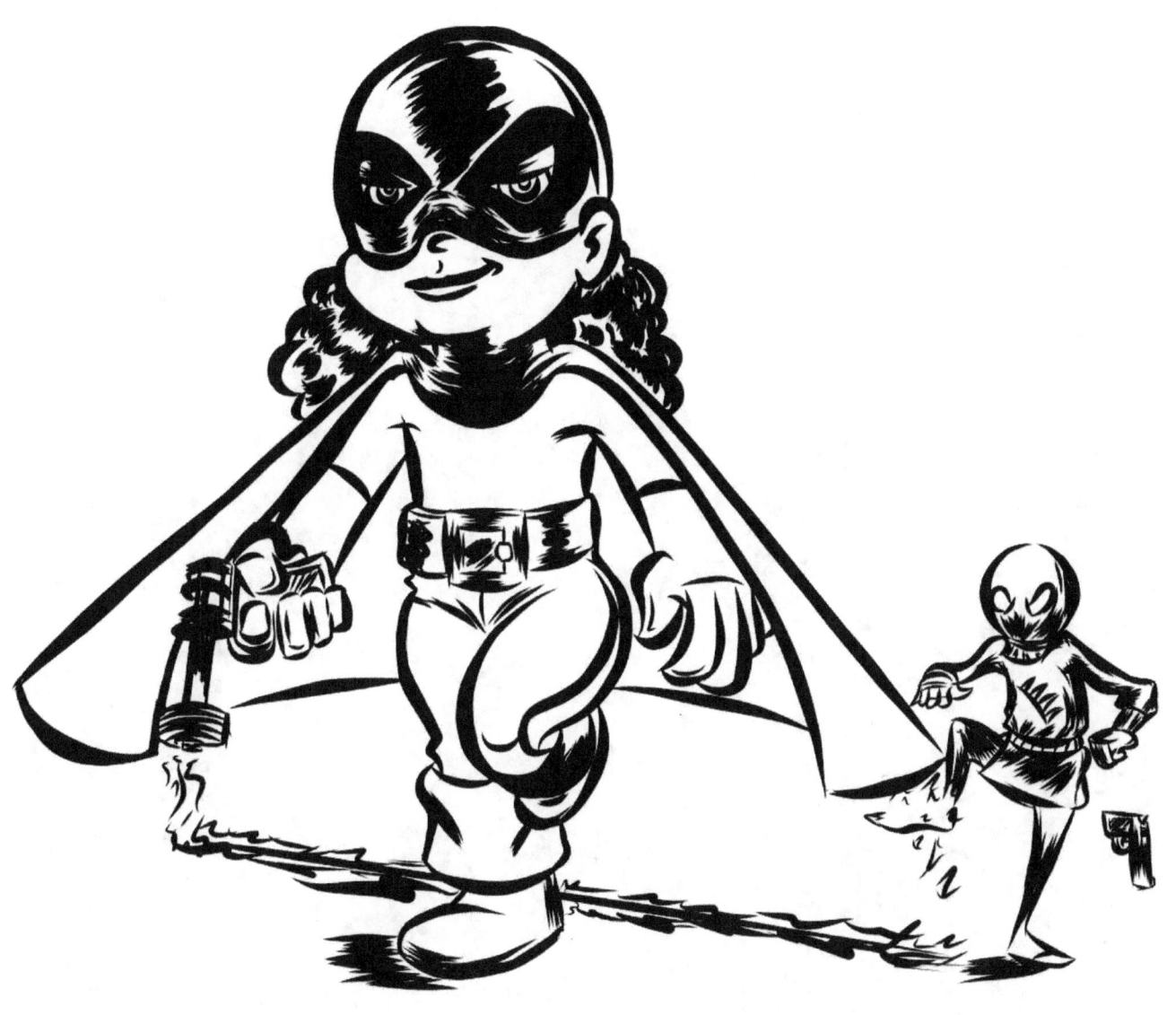

chiba 37

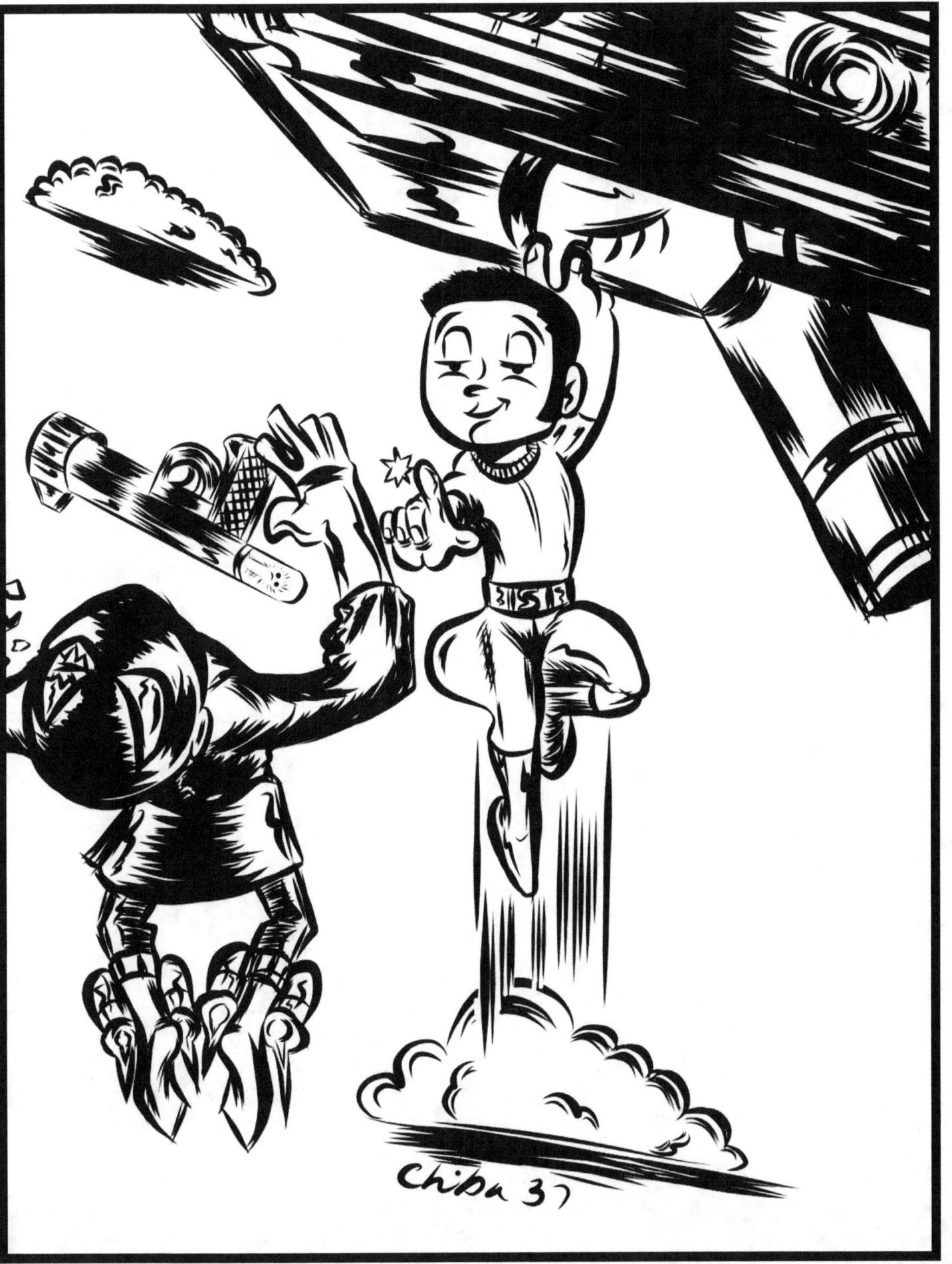

Chiba 37

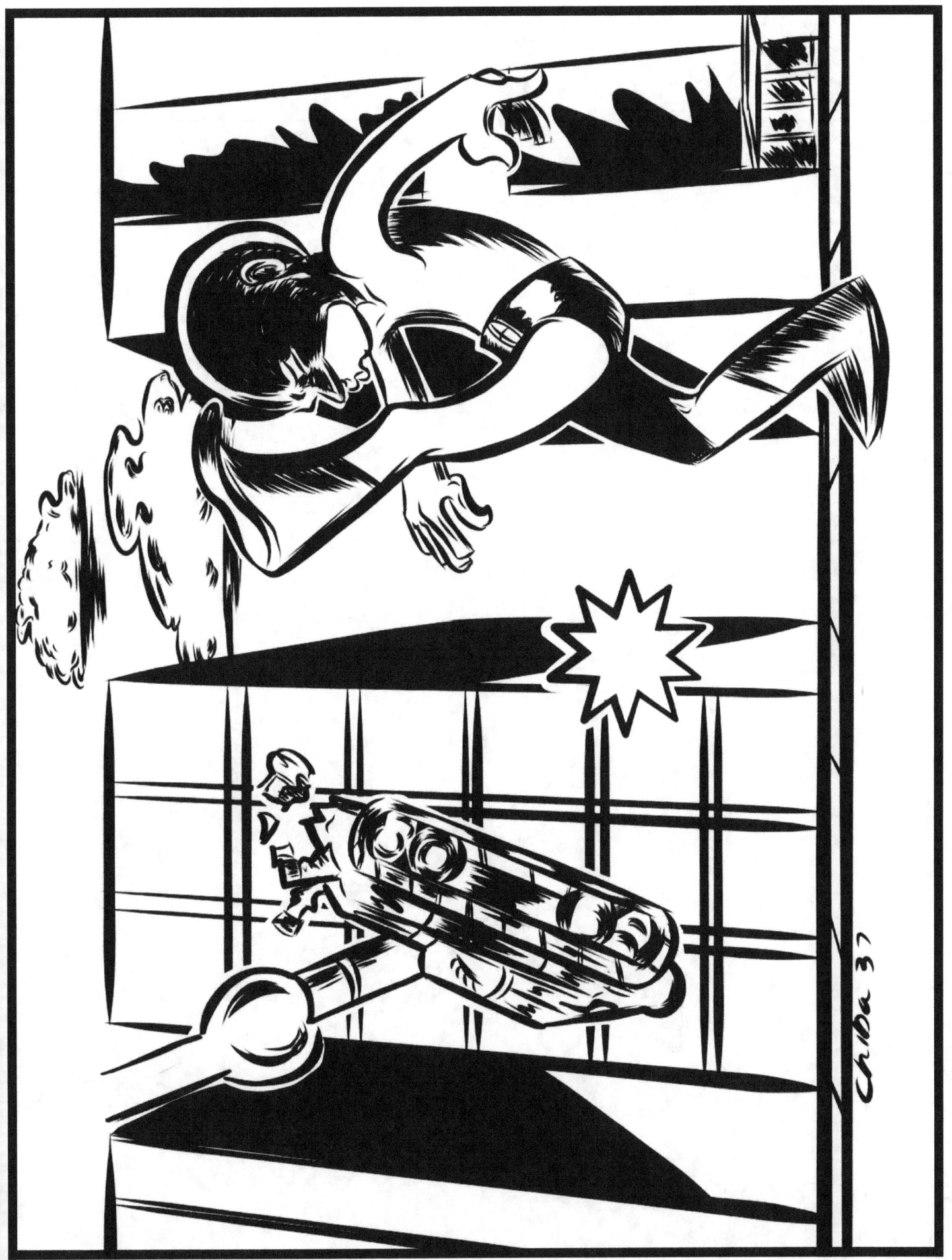

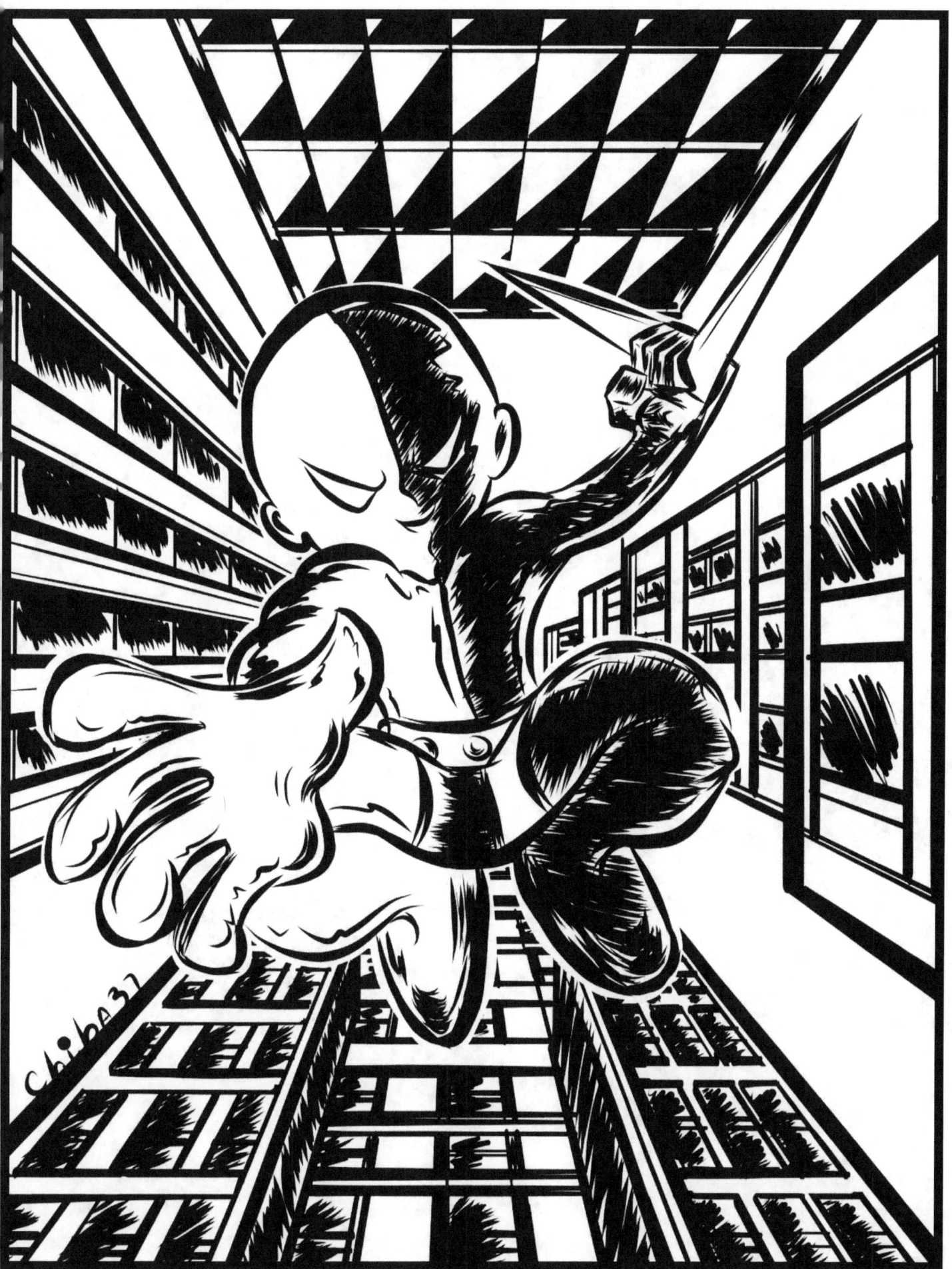

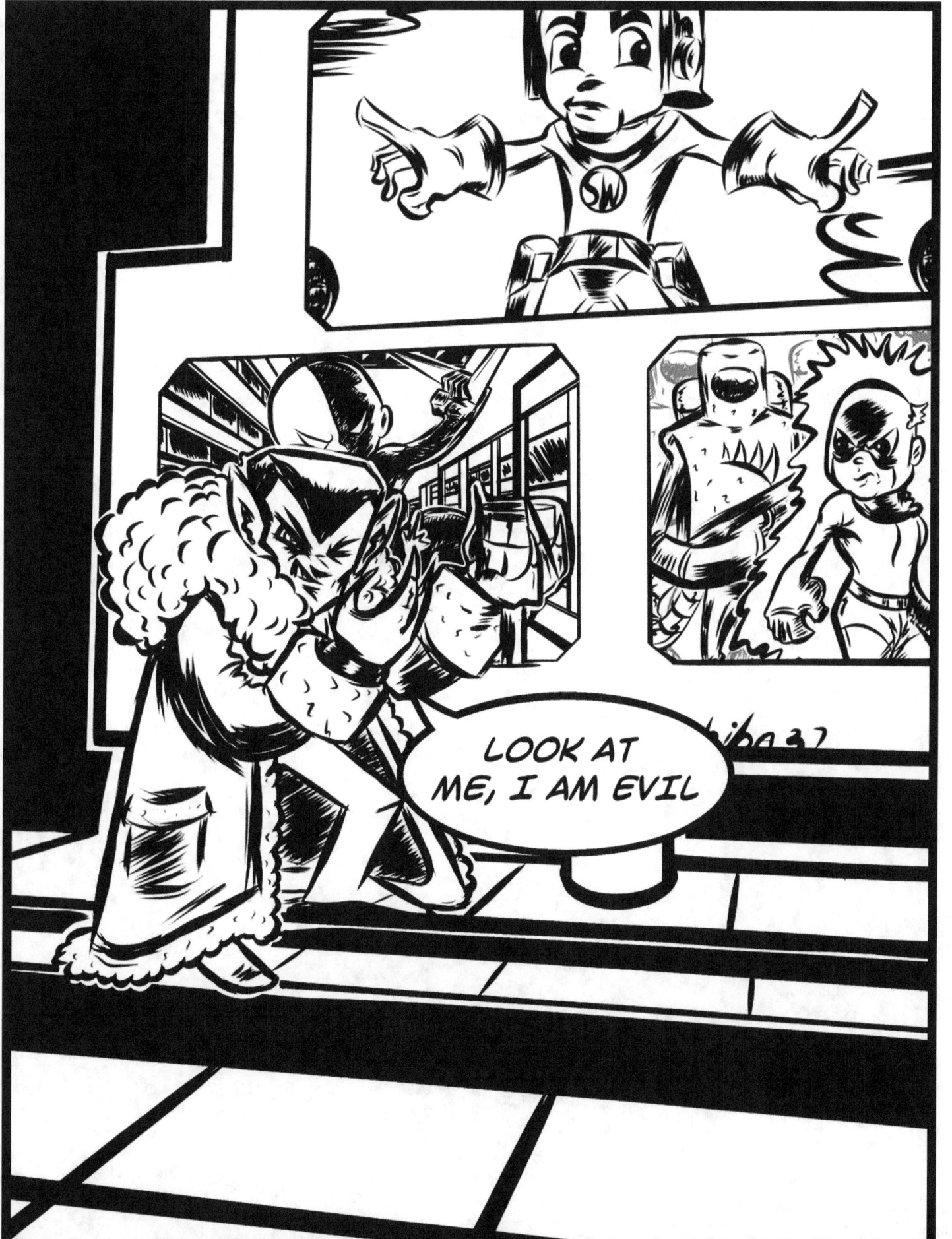

www.ingramcontent.com/pod-product-compliance
Lightning Source LLC
Chambersburg PA
CBHW081745220526

45468CB00008B/2252